REMEMBERING

FLORIDA'S FORGOTTEN COAST

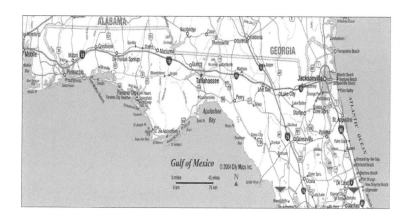

J. KENT THOMPSON

Copies can be ordered from the publisher at:
www.lulu.com\shop\

Note: While all the stories are true, some have been fictionalized to protect the identities and privacy of friends and fellow officers.

The reader is invited to share their "Forgotten Coast" memories with the author at jkt416@gmail.com, or join the Remembering Florida's Forgotten Coast facebook group @https://www.facebook.com/groups/681517521884732/

Front cover photo: a Steinhatchee sunset
Back cover photo: my granddaughter at Cape San Blas

2nd paperback edition

Acknowledgements

There are many people who deserve recognition for their assistance in writing this book. First and foremost are the people of the Forgotten Coast who allowed me to be a part of their lives.

Next are my fellow officers of the former Florida Marine Patrol and the current Fish and Wildlife Conservation Commission. I had the privilege to serve with some of the finest, most dedicated law enforcement officers in the world.

Thanks to Barbara Ohelbeck and John Foster, fellow writers and mentors whose edits and kind words encouraged me along the way. Thanks to Joe O'Shea, Director of the Center for Undergraduate Research and Academic Engagement at Florida State University for the grant which enabled me to further develop my stories. Dr. Jonathan Sheppard who served as my supervising professor and Mary Kozar, student advisor at Florida State University who helped me find venues to put my stories in the public's eye.

Special thanks to Adelaide Mitchell, English Professor at Tallahassee Community College for the many hours she spent with me in editing the book in its current form.

Finally thanks to my wife Janet for her patience and support of my efforts. I could never have written this book without her love and understanding.

Table of Contents

By J. Kent Thompson

FOREWORD

This book relates to stories about places in North Florida from Cedar Key to Panama City. As you read, you will learn about places named for the Spanish Saints, Florida seafood, and the people of an area called the "Forgotten Coast." [1]

The Forgotten Coast supposedly got its name in reaction to a slight from a tourism group that forgot to put information about the area in its publications. In retaliation a local group of businessmen created their own brochure and map calling the area the "Forgotten Coast". The

---

[1] The term Florida's Forgotten Coast is a registered trademark of the Apalachicola Bay Chamber of Commerce.

official "Forgotten Coast" is an area from the St. Marks Lighthouse in Wakulla County to Mexico Beach in Bay County.

Looking at the number of tourist spots on Florida's west coast it can easily be seen that there is a vast area between Panama City and Cedar Key that has been forgotten. I am referring to the areas ignored by developers and tourism councils. Those of us who have lived here or others who have regularly visited Northern Florida have always known that this area is the real Florida paradise. We just didn't want others to know.

Preface

This book is the result of a Mentored Research and Creative Endeavors Award (MRCE) I was received while attending Florida State University. I started my love affair with North Florida's coasts and its history as a child growing up in Tallahassee, Fl. After graduating from Leon High School in 1969, I joined the Marine Corps Reserves. After boot camp and specialized training I returned home to attend college. Being a solid "C" student at the time, I decided to leave school and seek a law enforcement career in natural resource protection. I was hired by the Florida Marine Patrol as an officer in 1972. For the next 37 years I lived and worked on both the east and west coasts of Florida. I retired at the rank of Major with the Florida Fish and Wildlife Conservation Commission in 2008 and decided to return to college in 2010. I graduated from FSU in 2013 *Magna Cum Laude* with a Bachelors degree in History and a minor in Religion. That is where this book came to fruition. My desire in this book is to give you a glimpse of living and working in one of the most beautiful places in the world, Florida's "Forgotten Coast." Included with the stories are some seafood recipes from my family and friends, as well as a few that were developed in the kitchen of the former state Board of Conservation. Hopefully as you read the stories you will not only get a taste of life on the "Forgotten Coast" but want to try some of its seafood as well.

JKT

CHAPTER ONE- FLORIDA HISTORY

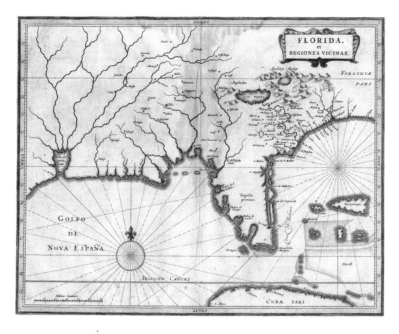

Florida 1640 by Joannes de Laet, State Archives of Florida

Florida has the longest recorded history of any state in the United States dating from Juan Ponce de Leon's landing in 1513. While it was the first land to be discovered in the new world, it was among the last to be settled and developed.[2] Today there are not too many native Floridians around, so for those who don't know anything about the State of Florida the following is a short course on Florida history. Hopefully it will enhance your enjoyment of the Sunshine State – there will be no test.

---

[2] Robert H. Gore, *The Gulf of Mexico*, (Sarasota: Pineapple Press 1992), 46

Early Indians in Florida

This land was originally inhabited by the first peoples to come to America, the Paleo-Indian, whose roots can be traced back to 12, 000 B.C.[3] By 5,000 B.C these native Indians had established settlements on the coasts, their livelihood depending on the shellfish found in the waters and wild game in the woods.

The earliest known Indian name for Florida was *Ikanayuksa* which meant "the land blessed by the Sun, Moon and (their children) the Stars: where the favoring rains, breezes, light and warmth of heaven make the harvests." [4] There is no better description of this state; we are surely blessed.

Prior to the white man coming to Florida's coasts it was called *Cautio* by the Lucayan Indians, a group of Indians who lived in the Bahamas and visited the area.[5] The reason they named it such was that the early inhabitants covered themselves with plaited palm leaves, but how that fact related to the name has been lost with their dialect.

First Spanish Occupation of Florida

When Spaniard Juan Ponce de Leon landed on Florida's northeast coast in 1513 there were five large Indian populations in Florida. The Timucua were in northeast and central, the Tequesta in the southeast, the Calusa in the southwest, the Tocobaga in the Tampa Bay area, and the

---

[3] Jerald T. Milanich, *Florida's Indians from Ancient Times to the Present* (Florida: University Press, 1998), 1
[4] Frank Drew, "Florida Place-Names of Indian Origin," *Florida Historical Society Quarterly* 6, no.4, (April 1928), 203
[5] J. Clarence Simpson, *A Provisional Gazetteer of Florida Place-Names of Indian Derivation* (Florida: Florida Geological Survey, Special Publication No. 1, 1956), 37

Apalachee in the Big Bend. Ponce de Leon renamed their land *La Florida* for its lush beauty and because it was the season of *Pascua Florida*, the Easter feast of flowers, and claimed it for Spain. He would be the first of many coming to the "new" land seeking her riches and renaming her coasts.

The explorer did not find a welcoming party when he arrived, landing near present day St. Augustine. The Timucua Indians there were stated to have been "fierce and warlike" and attacked his landing party. It's an ironic twist of today where visitors are welcomed in numerous "Visit Florida" commercials that the very first tourist to the east coast was not.[6] His reception in 1521 on the west coast was even less pleasant than his first as he was mortally wounded by the Calusa Indians when he tried to land. It seems those living on the lower west coast did not want to be discovered either but their actions guaranteed they'd never be forgotten.

The Spanish occupied Florida for the next 250 years. While the first permanent European settlement in America was established at St. Augustine in 1565, Spain did little more to colonize or develop the land. Under orders from King Phillip II, they did try to introduce their religion to the Indian population. The Franciscans built missions throughout the north Florida area (Florida's earliest bed and breakfasts) and many Indians were converted to Catholicism, but many also died from the white man's diseases.

In 1704 Englishman Colonel James Moore of South Carolina led attacks on the Spanish missions in Florida, burning them to the ground and slaughtering or enslaving the Apalachee Indians living there. The result was that for the next century the area lapsed into a wilderness worse

---

[6] Visit Florida is a non-profit corporation created by the Florida legislature in 1996 aimed at encouraging Florida tourism

than the Spanish explorers had found.[7] The original native tribes, which numbered about 350,000, were so decimated by tribal wars, slave trade, and disease that by the late 1760s only five hundred survived. [8]

British Rule in Florida

In 1763 Spain traded Florida to Britain for the return of Havana, which had been seized by the British during their Seven Years War. The British ruled Florida for the next 20 years colonizing the land more than any time it had been under Spain's control. The British divided the area into East and West Florida and established a governor for each.[9] Pensacola became the capital of West Florida and St. Augustine the capital of East Florida. The interior and southern area remained wild lands inhabited by the Indians.

----

[7] Malcomb B. Johnson, *Red, White, and Bluebloods in Frontier Florida*, (Tallahassee: Rotary Clubs of Tallahassee, 1976), 2
[8] Milanich, *Florida's Indians from Ancient Times to the Present*, viii : estimates of the Indian populations in pre-Columbian times are hard to determine but this one seems to best relay the numbers in 1513, though others have given estimates both higher and lower.
[9] It is interesting to note that the state was divided again in the 1950s. The informal division was of the northern and southern parts of the state with the "crackers who resided in the north and those "Damn Yankee tourists who were visiting Miami and Ft. Lauderdale in the south. The interior around Kissimmee and Orlando remained wild, soon to be inhabited by visitors seeking a large talking mouse and his friends. Both contributed to the creation of our Forgotten Coast.

Second Spanish Occupation of Florida

At the end of the Revolutionary War, Spain reclaimed the land from the British and ruled from 1781 to 1819. In the late 1700s two groups of Creek Indians, one speaking a dialect called Hitchiti and the other speaking Muskhogean now moved into North Florida. These Creeks, runaway slaves, members of remaining indigenous tribes, and Spanish settlers slowly began to move into the interior areas. Collectively they were called Seminoles; the name is either a corruption of the Creek *Ishti semoli* meaning "wild men", a name applied to separatists, "*Aulockawan*" which referred to where they lived, or a corruption of the Spanish word "*Cimarron*" which meant "wild or unruly."[10] They called the land "*Kanyuska*", meaning "lands end" and "end of it, or point" which refers to a peninsula. [11]Many of Florida's current place names are derivatives of their Hitchiti and Muskhogean languages. Colonists from the newly created United States also came, invited by Spain who wished to colonize and develop the land.

Spain was soon preoccupied with foreign wars and ruled Florida from a distance. The Seminoles attacked ships coming into Apalachicola as well as farms in Alabama and Georgia. American farmers took advantage of Spain's inability to defend the land by staging raids into Florida in search of runaway slaves and to retaliate for Seminole attacks on their farms. Soon both sides were burning each other's home sites and killing the inhabitants.[12]

---

[10] Simpson, *A Provisional Gazetteer of Florida Place-Names of Indian Derivation,* 98-99

[11] Ibid. 37: Simpson states that Minnie Moore Wilson reported that Florida was called this name by the Seminoles.

[12] Florida still has an annual invasion of farmers from Alabama and Georgia into the panhandle area, mainly into Panama City

In 1818 Andrew Jackson led a force against the Seminoles into Spanish-occupied Florida under the pretense of putting down their raids on American settlers and ships. He captured the town of Pensacola, the fort in St. Marks, and the Indian village at Suwannee Old Town. Jackson's men arrested two British nationals living with the Indians whom he accused of being spies. He said the men were supplying the Indians and runaway slaves with arms and ammunition, and inciting them to riot. The men, Alexander Arbuthnot and Robert Ambrister were quickly court marshaled and found guilty. Arbuthnot was hung and Ambrister faced a firing squad. Jackson then turned the captured cities back over to the Spanish and returned to New Orleans, but the incident had caused an international uproar and sparked what became known as Florida's First Seminole War.

Spain transfers Florida to the United States

Spain protested Jackson's invasion of Florida and the United States in return told them to either control the Seminoles or cede Florida to the U.S. Realizing they were too weak to defend the land, Spain eventually agreed to sign Florida over to the United States. Under the terms of the Adams-Onis Treaty of 1819, Spain ceded Florida to the United States.[13] A term of the transfer was that the United

---

which has led to it being called "The Redneck Riviera." While they do not kill, they do chase women, trash motels, lay drunk on the beaches and get burned. The Seminoles also still exist but in two distinct forms, the proud nation residing in the Everglades and the students in Tallahassee who like to mimic the farmers when they visit the coast.

[13] The treaty was negotiated by then United States Secretary of State John Quincy Adams and Spain's minister Luis de Onis on February 22, 1819 but was not ratified until February 22, 1821.

States agreed to settle American citizen's claims against Spain up to a sum of $5,000,000 dollars, about the cost of a fancy beach house on St. George Island today. It would take two years for the transfer to be completed.

Andrew Jackson was installed as Florida's first military governor in 1821 but only governed for eleven weeks before he left, at which time William P. Du Val became governor.

Many today question Jackson's handling of the Indians, especially when, as President, he had his friend James Gadsden negotiate the Treaties of Moultrie Creek in 1823 and Payne's Landing in 1832 which pushed the Seminoles further into the interiors of the land. The final insult was the Treaty of Fort Gibson in 1833 which forced all Indians to move west of the Mississippi which sparked Florida's Second Seminole War.

Springtime Tallahassee, an annual celebration of Florida's history and culture, celebrates Jackson's rule with a resident being chosen yearly to dress up as him and lead the parade, but not many of Seminole Indian descent cheer when he passes.

Florida as a United States Territory

In 1822 Florida's government was established by Congressional Act and formally recognized as a U.S. Territory. The total population of Florida at that time was about 12,000 with half that number being Indians. The land was as wild as it had been 250 years prior when the Spanish first claimed it. The majority of whites and blacks both slave and free were located in St. Augustine and Pensacola. The interior was occupied by Seminole Indians and their black slaves.

Desiring to become part of the United States, a constitutional convention was held in the coastal city of St. Joseph in 1838 to draft a document for statehood. It was not until seven years later in 1845, when the territory could insure the safety of settlers from Indian attacks, that it was granted statehood. In March of 1845 Florida became the twenty-seventh state in the union and hoisted what was called the "Mosley Flag" after Florida's governor William

P. Mosley.[14] Though the flag never was officially recognized it said a lot about how Floridians felt. Coincidentally Andrew Jackson, its first military Governor, died that same year.

Travel in Florida

Early travel across the territory was by way of old Indian or Spanish mission trails. To connect the missions and villages, the Spanish built a road called the El Camino Real which connected St. Augustine with the Tallahassee area.

In 1824 congress authorized Florida's first Federal Highway from St. Augustine to Pensacola following the route of the old Spanish trails, it was called the Bellamy Road, named for its architect.[15] Later, in 1900, the routes were revived and became what today is known as State Road 26. For the next 100 years Florida's population slowly grew and developed around these routes, but it was not until the land boom of the 1920s that her southern areas began to grow dramatically.

In 1831 Florida's first railroad charter was authorized from Tallahassee to Port Leon on the gulf coast, which opened in 1837 with its cars being drawn on wooden rails by mules[16]. Another railroad (actually the first steam

---

[14] The Mosley Flag was the unofficial flag of Florida after it became a state. It was flown at the inauguration of Governor William D. Mosley March 3, 1845

[15] John Bellamy of Monticello was contracted by Governor Du Val to build the eastern portion of the road from the Ochlocknee River to St. Augustine.

[16] The St. Marks Railroad operated from 1837 until 1959. The 16.2 railroad right of way was later converted in 1989 to Florida's first "rail to trail" where abandoned railway beds became hiking and biking trails.

powered railroad to open in Florida) started operations between St. Joseph and Lake Wimico in 1836. Both served to open the port areas to allow goods to pass from inland areas thereby effectively opening the gates to the North Florida coasts. The railroads brought prosperity to "Middle Florida," that area from the Georgia border to the gulf, and encompassing from the Apalachicola River to the Suwannee River. They also brought settlers and the next thirty years saw the population of the area swell to contain 50% of Florida's population. Such drastic change and growth would not come to the North Florida areas again until the completion of Interstate 10 in 1978.

Early Tourism to the Forgotten Coast

Tourism came to the coastal areas in the 1800s in the form of visitors to Wakulla, Franklin, Gulf and Bay counties. They came by train or steamer to bath in the mineral springs at Panacea and Newport and play at the resorts of Lanark, St. Joseph and Teresa. To the inhabitants of the coast tourism was looked upon as a good source of income as one Florida Cracker said, "In the winter we live on the Yankee and in the summer on fish."[17] Tallahassee families also trekked to the beaches to picnic, swim and fish, some staying all summer which continues today. My family was no exception. We spent every opportunity swimming, fishing, hunting, and boating at nearby rivers and beaches.

Meanwhile, the people of the Forgotten Coast minded their business and raised their families, enjoying the bounty of the sea and the beauty of the woodlands. Today one can visit the sites where the early Indians lived, the

---

[17] Federal Writers Project, *American Guide Series: Florida: A Guide to the Southernmost State*, (New York: Oxford University Press, 1939), 129

explorers landed and the colonists settled. These reminders of our history help to make stories of the Forgotten Coast come alive.

The Coast

I have always looked forward to going to the coast. It was not until becoming an adult, traveling around the country, that I found the coast was known by other names. In the northeast they refer to it as *going down to the shore* and in the west it's *the beach*. We, in North Florida, have always known that you have to *first go to the coast to get to the beach*. Once you are at the beach then you can walk *to the shore*.

The coast of North Florida has many names, some were created as marketing tools by hopeful Chambers of Commerce such as Panama City's "World's Most Beautiful Beaches," Taylor County's "Nature Coast" or St. Joe's "Great Northwest."[18]

Some knew the area by its geographic characteristics which bring to mind a panhandle which explains it moniker the Panhandle or the Big Bend. Local place names have come from the Indians such as Wakulla, Steinhatchee, and Sopchoppy. Other names have come from those who operated resorts or had major land ownership in the area. Families like the Wilsons and Keaton's gave their own names to their beaches.

The Spanish explorers named many areas after their saints honoring St. Mark, St George, St. Vincent and San Blas.[19] Landmarks also lent their features to the names

---

[18] Each of these names were developed to market the areas to tourists

[19] Robert C. Galgano, *Feast of Souls*, (New Mexico: University of New Mexico Press, 1970), 47 -Part of the Spanish colonization efforts was to rename the Indian villages after their saints to

denoting a Stump Hole, Alligator Point, Grass Island, or Deadman's Bay. [20]

No matter what one may call an area, all together they form the Forgotten Coast. It is the memories of these places that make up these stories.

CHAPTER TWO- LEON COUNTY

Leon County

Leon County was named for the Spanish explorer, Juan Ponce De Leon.[21] Tallahassee, the capital of Florida, is located in Leon County. The city is located 14 miles from the Georgia border and 20 miles from the Gulf of Mexico. It was chosen as the location for the state capital after two emissaries of Florida's Territorial government were sent to find a suitable location midway between the eastern and western extremes of the territory to build a capital.[22]

In June of 1823 Colonel John Lee Williams traveled from Pensacola, the capital of West Florida, by way of water and came into St. Marks. There he met with Dr. William H. Simmons who had traveled by land on horseback from St. Augustine, the capital of East Florida. Together they went to the location of a former Apalachee Indian village called *Osaceila* now known as Tallahassee. The name is from the Creek word for town "*Talawa*" and "*Ahassee*" meaning "old". Together they meant "old town or old or abandoned fields" in memory of the former Apalachee settlement that had been there.[23] Arriving near today's Cascades Park

---

[21] Allen Morris, *Florida Place Names* (Florida: Pineapple Press, 1995), 147.

[22] Prior to the establishment of the city of Tallahassee in 1824, the main population centers in Florida were in Pensacola and St. Augustine. The Apalachicola River was the dividing line between East and West Florida

[23] J. Clarence Simpson, *A Provisional Gazetteer of Florida Place-Names of Indian Derivation* (Florida: Florida Geological Survey, Special Publication No. 1, 1956), 103

they found a spot they felt would be suitable for the capital building.[24]

The city of Tallahassee was established in 1824 and later that year the first Territorial Council meeting was held in a log cabin built for that purpose. By choosing Tallahassee as the territorial capital, a new economic area called Middle Florida was created. It encompassed the old Apalachee Indian lands south from the Georgia border to the Suwannee River and west to the Apalachicola River. It was from here in this newly created area that the early history of Florida would emanate.

Tallahassee

Tallahassee, from its establishment in 1824 until Florida statehood in 1845, was known as a wild and dangerous place to live. Congress, wishing to reward the Marques de Lafayette for his assistance in the Revolutionary War, had granted him a 24,000 acre township in the new city but he never settled there, choosing instead to sell off parcels to pay his debts. The housing was primitive and the streets were daily filled with fights and drunkards. Law enforcement was lax, there was not even a secure jail established until 1836.[25]

Political immigrants from Virginia, South Carolina, Kentucky and Tennessee sought fame and fortune in the new land boom area called Florida. Many would find

---

[24] Cascades Park is located south of the current capitol building. Renamed Centennial Field when Tallahassee reached its centennial year, it has been the home for a minor league baseball team and was the location of Florida State University's football team first game. It now is a city park and bandstand.

[25] Malcomb B. Johnson, *Red, White and Bluebloods in Frontier Florida,* (Tallahassee: Florida, Rotary Clubs of Tallahassee, 1976), 12.

favor and would leave their marks as Governors and representatives of the new territory and later state. As the city filled with new citizens and politicians it gained a reputation of "vice, intemperance, gambling, and profanity."[26] A New Englander named John Tappan had written a letter to his friend commenting on how one "could not walk the streets without being armed to the teeth."[27] In 1840 troops were even called in to restore order in the city.[28] Things began to change in 1841 when a yellow fever epidemic hit the city and wiped out many of the ruffians as well as some upstanding citizens, filling the plots of the Old City Cemetery. A fire swept through the town in 1843 and most of its downtown wood structures were destroyed. As the city began to rebuild an ordinance was passed to require masonry construction. A new Tallahassee rose from the ashes and soon became the center of commerce.

Plantations with names like Wacissa and Lipona sprang up on the surrounding lands and soon wagonloads of cotton and other goods from North Florida and South Georgia traveled down tree laden canopy roads that still exist today.[29] Once in the city, goods were transported by rail to the port of St. Marks to be shipped to markets around the country.

---

[26] W.T. Cash, *Florida Becomes a State*, (Tallahassee: Florida Centennial Commission, 1945), 17.

[27] Ibid.,19

[28] Ibid.,19

[29] Tallahassee has five canopy roads; Centerville, Meridian, Miccosukee, Old Bainbridge and Old St. Augustine. Wacissa was a plantation in Jefferson County started by Col. James Gadsden and Prince Murat. Murat later moved to his own plantation calling it Lipona

The Lynching of Mick Morris

Tallahassee started out as a place for ruffians and politicians (I am not sure if the terms are not interchangeable.) Regardless, its past had hidden secrets that some would prefer not to be revealed. One such secret was the truth about the lynching of Mick Morris. It was in 1983 when my step-father, Hayward Atkinson[30], finally told me his family's deepest and darkest secret—his Uncle Clyde had been part of a lynch mob that had murdered a man. It had occurred in 1909, when Clyde was all of eight years old. His father had awakened him one June night and told him he needed to come with him to see what was going to happen. Clyde's mother had protested but knew she could not change her husband's mind. So Clyde loaded onto a wagon with his father and some other "concerned citizens" of Leon County as they went to carry out their vigilante justice.

The events that led up to that night had their roots in the murder of Leon County's Sheriff Willie M. Langston in March of 1909.[31] Langston, who happened to be a family relative, was killed apprehending an escaped convict. The convict, Mick Morris, had escaped from a Georgia jail and was reported to be hiding at a turpentine camp at Springhill in southern Leon County. As my step-father relayed it to me Sheriff Langston went to the camp and asked where Morris was, he was told that he was hiding in one of the camp shacks. Sheriff Langston went to the shack and called for Morris to come out and give himself up. Unknown to the Sheriff, Morris armed with a shotgun, was

---

[30] All references in this book that speak of my "father" refer to my step-father Hayward Atkinson.
[31] Langston would be the only Leon County Sheriff's department officer killed in the line of duty for the next 105 years until the ambush and murder of Deputy Chris Smith Nov 22, 2014.

hiding under the shack. When the Sheriff approached the steps of the shack, Morris shot him and escaped. Sheriff Langston, mortally wounded, was rushed back to Tallahassee but died on the steps to the hospital. Morris meanwhile fled back to Georgia. A warrant was sworn out for Morris's arrest and he was extradited back to Tallahassee where he was tried and convicted of Sheriff Langston's murder. His sentence was death by hanging, to be carried out on June 11, 1909.

Here is where Clyde and the men riding on the wagon came into the story. Around town, people were upset that it had taken so long for justice to be served. A rumor was going around that Morris had been acting like he was insane to avoid the gallows. For reasons unknown, on June 6, 1909 the citizens decided to take matters into their own hands.

A reported group of fifteen men went to the jail and banged on the door. They advised the jailer inside they were going to take his prisoner. Opening the door, the jailer gave the men his keys and put his hands behind his back to be tied, telling the men he "wished they wouldn't do that." Morris, upon seeing the mob at his cell door, fought for his life. To subdue him, one of the men shot him in the left arm. They then dragged him out of the cell, threw a rope over the oak tree outside the jail and hung him. At the time the Leon County Jail was located on the corner of Gaines and Meridian Streets just blocks away from the capital building. A photograph was taken of Morris's body hanging in the tree; to the side is the wagon-load of men who had done the deed, Clyde among them.

As a child I saw the photograph often. My step-father had made a copy of it and framed it, resting the frame on a shelf beneath his gun rack. But I never knew the story behind it. So why in 1983 did I finally find out? It was only because that is when Clyde died — the last surviving member of the vigilante lynch mob that had hung Mick

Morris. Clyde had grown up and ironically become a defense attorney. He had a long, successful career and through the years had become a millionaire. But one thing he could never escape was the fact that he had been part of a group that had committed a murder, something of which there was no statute of limitations in Florida. So the secret has been kept--until now.

Hanging Tree on Gaines Street by old City Jail

Blue Sink, photo by author

Blue Sink Klan

Sinkholes are a common occurrence in the Forgotten
Coast because the ground contains limestone, an easily
dissolvable rock. When groundwater flows through these
rocks, it eats away at them, leaving behind subterranean
holes and caverns. When the roof of one of these caverns
collapses, it takes the land above down with it forming a
sinkhole. Blue Sink is such a sinkhole located just outside
Tallahassee on the Wakulla Springs road. It is closed to the
public now, but when I was a kid we spent many
weekends swimming there. The sink was small in
comparison to others in the area, maybe about 200 yards in
circumference. The waters were silky blue which is how it
got its name. It has a sandy beach where kids could play
and picnickers eat or sunbathe. The sink was situated
down an embankment that allowed us to drive our car up

to its banks anywhere around it and peer down on the swimmers.

One weekend we were at the sink with my mother and a friend of hers and her kids. We had a picnic planned and had brought three cannonball watermelons for dessert. Mom placed the watermelons in the shallow water of the spring near the beach so they could cool while we swam.

About 11 o'clock, while we were swimming and my mom and her friend were sitting on the beach, about 14 cars pulled up all at once. My mother looked at her friend and us anxiously as she did not know what to expect. The occupants of the cars just sat there for what seemed like an eternity. We stood in the water, watching the cars, then our mother, wondering what was going on and what we should do. Suddenly the doors opened and people dressed in robes started getting out and walking towards us. I was sure we were going to be killed for swimming at a place where the local Ku Klux Klan had decided to meet. [32]

As the Klan members at Blue Sink got out of their cars we looked intently at their faces. They were not wearing hoods and upon closer inspection we saw they were black. The men and women came down the banks of the sink and one of them, a preacher, started praying. What we had thought was a gathering of the Klan turned out to be a church group gathering for baptism.

The preacher called individuals up to him, and after speaking to each one, dunked him or her in the water saying "In the name of the Father, Son, and Holy Ghost, I claim you as a child of the Lord". We watched in amazement. I had never seen an open air baptism before that day.

---

[32] The Klu Klux Klan or KKK was prevalent in the south. Its goal was to promote white supremacy and intimidate minorities; they were adamantly against the civil rights laws of the 1960s.

I noticed that they were being baptized in the shallow end of the water where our watermelons floated. Each time a "brother" or "sister" went under the water, our watermelons bobbed right along with them. Everyone was shouting and singing and those who had been baptized were praising the Lord.

Then as quickly as they had started, they went back to their cars smiling, laughing and calling to one another as they were leaving. We started mimicking the baptisms, dunking each other and saying" Hallelujah!" Later we gathered up the melons and ate our picnic lunch. We could not help but laugh when we thought about the baptized melons bobbing in the holy water as we enjoyed the "blessed" fruit.

At the time I didn't know too much about the Ku Klux Klan except what you heard around town, but I knew enough to be afraid. It was years later when I was 15, that I and a friend of mine were introduced to the face of the Klan. His older brother had a driver's license and whenever their parents went out of town, he would disconnect the speedometer and we'd drive their family car around town.

One night we were cruising down Monroe Street in front of the Florida Theater when we saw some men throwing flyers out the window of their car to passer-bys on the sidewalk.[33] We stopped and picked one up. It read "The American Monkey" and had a picture of a black man hanging from a tree. Below it was the caption "The only good nigger." I noticed that the language in the pamphlet was ignorant and many words were misspelled. It invited everyone to come to the cross burning in a field behind the Seminole Truck stop on West Tennessee Street. My friend's brother decided he wanted to go and since he was driving we rode along.

When we got there we saw cars lined up in a semi-circle across the field. There was a huge 35 foot cross wrapped in oily cloths in the center. The car headlights provided light on a makeshift stage where a man was standing dressed in a hood and robe with scarlet markings. He had a microphone in his hand and was talking to a gathering of similarly dressed men, women and children around the stage. Actually, he was ranting more than talking. He denigrated the entire "negro" race and any white people who would intermingle with them, calling them white trash and their children mulatto's.[34] It did not take us long to realize that we did not want to stick around and hear too much more of his rancor. But being kids, we were interested in seeing the cross burning, so we hung around a little longer.

----

[33] Monroe Street is the main north and south thoroughfare through the city of Tallahassee.

[34] Mulatto was a term used to describe persons of mixed or biracial ancestry.

Cross burning at nighttime Ku Klux Klan (KKK) rally,
Photo by Hank Walker, 1946, Time Life

Finally, the people gathered around the stage went back
to their cars and turned off their car lights. A robed man
with a torch went up to the cross and set it afire. The
flames shot up and over the cross in a burst of yellow and
orange burning brightly in the quiet, darkened field. I just
stared at it, not knowing what to think. At the time I didn't
know what the burning cross meant (the Klan used it to
intimidate and terrorize people) but I knew this was not
representative of the cross I saw in church on Sunday.
Looking back, that was a coming of age event for me as I
had not seen the ugly side of racism until then.

The End of Innocence

Growing up in North Florida we never worried too much about crime until a series of murders occurred in 1966 and 1967. The first, known as the "Sims Murders" changed the way we lived.

One cool October night in 1966, the Sims were at home listening to a Florida State football game with their daughter, Joy, while their two other daughters Jenny and Judy, were out babysitting.[35] Sometime during the evening, an intruder, who many thought knew the family, came to their door. He gained entry into the house then pulled a gun and ordered the husband to tie up his wife and child and then the intruder tied him up as well. After the family was bound, Mr. and Mrs. Sims were shot. Joy was sexually molested then shot and stabbed repeatedly. Jenny returned home to find her father and sister dead and her mother barely holding on to life. Mrs. Sims lingered for a few days before succumbing to her wounds. She was never able to identify their attacker.

Tallahassee grew-up that night. People who had never locked their doors started doing so and there was an increase on gun and lock sales at local stores. Halloween was coming up the following week and it was strongly suggested that kids stay inside rather than going door-to-door wearing masks.[36]

It seemed that bad news kept arriving. A week later the body of salesman R.W. Bittinger was pulled from Blue Sink.[37] Sheriff officials started checking into the case and found that Bittinger lived about a mile away from the Sims

---

[35] Ed Sherer, "Man, Daughter Slain, Wife Listed Critical," *Tallahassee Democrat* ,October 23, 1966

[36] "Not Tonight, Please!" *Tallahassee Democrat* ,October 31, 1966

[37] "Body Found in Blue Sink," *Tallahassee Democrat* ,October 31, 1966

northwestern Tallahassee home. Could he have been a link to their murders? His wife said he had been depressed before his death, which occurred on the date of their wedding anniversary. If he was involved it was never proven but Blue Sink, a popular spot for lovers to park, was soon in the news again.

It was almost exactly a year later, October 17, 1967, when another gruesome murder rocked the county. It was at the same site where R.W. Bittinger was found-- Blue Sink.

This time it was the scene of a grisly double murder. Two teenage girls, Ann Wood and Kay Granger, both 17, had gone riding with a man that Kay Granger used to date and during the night things turned terribly wrong.[38] Around 11:30 that night the Tallahassee Police Department got an anonymous call from a man reporting two bodies at Blue Sink. Sheriff's deputies rushed to the scene and found the battered remains of the two girls.[39] Both had been beaten in the head with a blunt instrument, stabbed and shot. Ann Wood's body was partially clad in her undergarments and it appeared she had been molested. Kay Granger's body was still fully clothed. The crime scene was combed for clues but not too many were found. An all points bulletin was put out in the area asking for any information about anyone who might look like they had been in a fight.

The next day the Leon County Sheriff got a call from his counterpart in Madison County.[40] The Sheriff in Madison County had a man at the local hospital that had come in

---

[38] Jim Hardee, "Friend Testifies Slain Girl's Picture Kept By Sanders," *Tallahassee Democrat*, February 9, 1968
[39] "Two Girls Found Hacked To Death Near Blue Sink," *Tallahassee Democrat* ,October 18, 1967
[40] Jim Hardee, "Friend Testifies Slain Girl's Picture Kept By Sanders," *Tallahassee Democrat*, February 9, 1968

with a gunshot wound and wanted to know if the Leon County Sheriff would like to question him. The Sheriff hurried over to Madison and after interviewing the man identified as Robert Scott Sanders, a drifter from California who was AWOL from the Army, he felt he had enough cause to hold him.

Sanders had told the Sheriff two different stories about how he had been shot.[41] At first he said it was an accidental shooting by a friend when he was cleaning his gun; the second involved a wild story about a fight with two men who had some girls in their car screaming for help on the road to Blue Sink.

Sanders, who had been in the north Florida area for a couple months, was working at a gas station in Madison as an attendant. A check was done on his whereabouts for the past year and it was soon found that he had been living in Tallahassee when the Sims murder had occurred. Was he a serial killer preying on Tallahassee residents? The guns used were different, a 38 caliber in the Sims murder and a 22 caliber in the Blue Sink murders but that did not mean he could not have been the killer. Did he know Bittinger? Was there some connection between his death and Sanders?

As Sanders murder trial began in February of 1968, Blue Sink was in the news again. The body of A.D. Landrum, who lived in northwest Tallahassee approximately 3 miles from the Sims home, was pulled from the water.[42] Could this be another grisly link to Sanders, Bittinger and the Sims murders? If so, nothing was ever done to try to link the deaths.

---

[41] Ibid.,
[42] "Local Man Drowns At Blue Sink," *Tallahassee Democrat* , February 8, 1968

At Sanders' trial, he admitted he had taken the girls to Blue Sink to go parking.[43] That night he probably had figured he was lucky to have two young girls riding with him. He went to the sink with intentions of satisfying his sexual passion and ended up committing two grisly murders. When they teased him and resisted his advances he said he got "teed off" at them and just snapped.[44] The girls fought back but he shot, stabbed and hacked them to death in his rage. Ann Woods had been stabbed over 60 times and both girls' skulls were crushed.

When pictures of the crime were introduced into evidence, one juror asked to be excused because they were so graphic.[45] The defense attorney argued that while Sanders had committed the crimes, he was not guilty because he was temporarily insane at the time they occurred. The prosecutor argued Sanders' knew exactly what he was doing, pointing to Sanders' precise recollections of the facts which proved he was aware of what happened that night.[46]

After deliberating for two and a half hours, the jury came back with a verdict of not guilty by reason of insanity.[47] Some members said there was no doubt he was guilty, only that a sane person could not do such a grisly thing. All agreed he needed to be kept away from society in the insane asylum at Chattahoochee.

[43] Jim Hardee, "Attorney Admits Sanders "Did It," *Tallahassee Democrat*, February 10, 1968
[44] Jim Hardee, "Oral Confession Made, Joyce Says," *Tallahassee Democrat*, February 9, 1968
[45] Jim Hardee, "Killings Were Crimes Of Passion-Hopkins," *Tallahassee Democrat* , February 8, 1968
[46] Ibid.,
[47] Jim Hardee, "Sanders Not Guilty In Blue Sink Slaying," *Tallahassee Democrat*, February 11, 1968

Blue Sink was closed by the Forest Service and today cars are blocked from entering the grounds. Visitors can get out at the gate and walk into the area to view the springs but it's not recommended to go at night because they might run into ghosts or even a murderer revisiting the scene of his crime.

Eight years after Sanders commitment he was released and deemed cured.[48] The Sims murder still remains unsolved today as well as the questions concerning Bittinger, Landrum, and Sanders.[49] Robert Scott Sanders was released to a halfway house in Pensacola in 1974 and later surfaced working as a security guard and carrying a gun.[50] The courts intervened as a matter of public safety and he was returned to the mental hospital in 1975. In April of 1976 he was released and allowed to move to Alaska to live with his parents.

Although these memories are of some bad times, they saw me and the people of the area come of age; they make me cling even harder to the good memories I have of the Forgotten Coast.

---

[48] Malcolm Johnson," Who's Responsible for the Irresponsible?" in *I Declare!*,(Tallahassee: Tallahassee Democrat, 1983), 1975
[49] With the December 2014 passing of Leon County Sheriff Larry Campbell, one of the first on the scene that night, any chance to ever find the Sims killer has probably been lost.
[50] *Daytona Beach Morning Journal*, April 3, 1975

CHAPTER THREE- WAKULLA COUNTY

Will-kill-ya County

Wakulla County (or Will-kill-ya County as it's jokingly called by some of the locals) was created in 1843 and named after its largest natural spring, Wakulla Springs. The county seat was originally established in Port Leon, but when the town was destroyed by a hurricane it was moved to Newport. When that city declined, it was moved to Crawfordville. Wakulla County is the gateway to the beaches of the north Florida coast.

The name Wakulla came from the Indian languages of its early inhabitants. Some say the name came from the Spanish spelling and Indian pronunciation of a Timucuan Indian word. The Spanish word *Guacara* was pronounced "Wakulla" by the Indians. Others say it comes from the Creek Indian word for loon, *wahkol*. [51]

The woods and water of Wakulla County have always been her riches. Loggers have taken timber for the naval stores and turpentine, bee-keepers have tended their hives, worm baiters and hunters have roamed the woods, and fishermen have plied her waters.

Today enterprising roadside businessmen sell tupelo honey, watermelons and hot boiled peanuts while traveling artists offer velvet Elvis paintings for sale out of the back of their vans.

Tourists continue to come to Wakulla County beaches and springs as they did in the 1800s and many have decided to call it their home. Recent tax rolls have swelled due to expensive residences in Crawfordville and beach homes in Dickerson Bay. Schools and government services have improved as a result. Once thought of as nothing but

---

[51] Simpson, *A Provisional Gazetteer of Florida Place-Names of Indian Derivation*, 123

woods and sand hills, the area is now a growing bedroom community for workers from Tallahassee seeking the simple life at an affordable price.

St. Marks

Centuries before the first explorers came to Florida in the 1500s, the Apalachee Indians had established the village of *Aute* near the mouth of the St. Marks River.[52] Spanish explorer's such as Panfilo de Narvaez and Hernando de Soto ventured into the area, but it was not until 1718 that Captain Jose Primo de Rivera came and established the first town of St. Marks. He named the town after the feast day of St. Mark.[53] Under orders from the Spanish governor of Florida he constructed a wooden fort, the Fort San Marcos de Apalache, overlooking the confluence of the St. Marks and Wakulla Rivers. A stone fort was begun on the site in 1739 but took years to finish. When the fort was acquired by the United States in 1821 it was alternately used as a garrison and a yellow fever hospital.

The city of St. Marks, established in 1828 as a major port on the Apalachee Bay, is one of five former port communities in the area. The others are Rock Haven (1826), Magnolia (1827), Port Leon (1839) and Newport (1843). Cotton, tobacco, timber, naval stores (products produced from the resin of pine trees such as tar, pitch and turpentine), and seafood were shipped from the port of St. Marks. Today it serves as a port for fuel oil.

---

[52] Paul E. Hoffman, *Florida's Frontiers* (Indiana: Indiana University Press, 2002) 31.
[53] Morris, *Florida Place Names*, 214

The St. Marks Lighthouse

St. Marks Lighthouse authors photo

I used to go to St. Marks Lighthouse on weekends to boat, crab and scallop. Construction of the first lighthouse was begun in 1829 and completed in 1831. Legend has it that stones from the old San Marcos de Apalache Fort located six miles north were used in its construction. The lighthouse was originally built to a height of 65 feet but after being damaged in the Civil War it was repaired and raised to 73 feet. The lighthouse was only accessible by water until a road leading to it was built by African American members of the Civilian Conservation Corps and completed in 1936-37. The lighthouse stands today as a lonely sentry guarding the Forgotten Coast as a part of the St. Marks National Wildlife Refuge.[54]

The Refuge is one of the forgotten coasts secrets. In the summer and fall the groundsel bushes around the lighthouse attract migrating monarch butterflies. As a child I remember how they would swarm around you, lighting on your hands and head. Hiking trails lead families to outdoor adventures where nature can be enjoyed as it was in years gone by. In the muddy ditches lining the lighthouse road one can see alligators basking in the sun. In the wintertime varieties of migrating birds come to the rookeries in the area to rest and feed, a way-station on their journey to Mexico, Central, and South America. In January the annual escort of the whooping cranes to the refuge is a sight to see.[55]

When I was young, you could climb to the top of the lighthouse and view the bay and surrounding rivers. Looking out at the shallow waters of the flats you could see the fine leaved turtle grasses being fanned by the calm gulf waters creating a safe refuge for blue-eyed scallops. Below you, Pelicans in loose v-formations fly low over the water. Green tidal marsh grasses marking snake-like bends in the river channels curve slowly to the gulf. The surrounding tidal marsh is filled with the alternating colors of deep black rush grasses and the bright greens and grays of cord grass. Oyster bars, serving as buffet tables for hungry raccoons rise up near the channel edges. Blue

---

[54] The 70, 000 acre St. Marks National Wildlife Refuge was established in 1931. It is located off of US 98 in Newport. After crossing the St. Marks River heading east, turn right onto Lighthouse road to get to the welcome center.
[55] Called Operation Migration, whooping cranes raised in captivity are escorted south by an ultra light pilot acting as a surrogate parent along a planned migration route from Wisconsin to Florida.

Herons, ducks and wading birds dive for fish in the tidal pools. Atop higher plots of distant lands, drought resistant pine hammocks mixed with sable and cabbage palms are visible. Black Mullet, being chased by hungry dolphins charge through the water churning it to white foam. A bald eagle sits atop a pine tree surveying his area. Then off in the distance the two rivers merge into murky brown syrup. Standing there I would watch as the day slowly faded into evening as the sun sank below the horizon in brilliant colors of deep reds, oranges, and purples. Then as if in a last hurrah, the marsh would come alive with the calling of sea birds, hawks and osprey returning to their roosts.

Today only the lighthouse keeper's home is opened to the public on the first Saturday of the month. Coming construction will see it closed until repairs can be made but then it should reopen for four days a week. Someday soon people may again have the opportunity to climb the lighthouse's winding staircase and experience the same wonder of the forgotten coast that drew me to her years ago. If so, I recommend you make the climb for it is a memory you will hold forever.

Scalloping

The flats, a shallow grassy area just off the lighthouse, were a great place to find delicious blue-eyed scallops. I would pull an inner-tube or the boat behind me and scout for the scallops lying on the thick sea grasses. It would not take long to find a hundred or more, then I would clean them right there on the water.

If you have ever taken scallops home to clean and had the smell of rotting viscera and shells around for awhile, you would understand why it's best to clean them on the water. In later years I learned a great trick about cleaning scallops at home, use a shop-vacuum. After opening the scallop shell just suck out the viscera with the vacuum hose. One side of the shell contains the meat and the vacuum will take away the guts while leaving the meat intact. It really works well. After you've finished, dump the waste in the trash and clean the shop-vacuum with a solution of bleach and water.

I also liked to crab in waters of the impoundment area by the lighthouse. I would take chicken necks and tie them to a fishing pole, then cast the line in the water and wait for the crabs to start feeding. When I felt a gentle tug I'd slowly reel them in and put them in my cooler. Crabs are cooked live and they always try to claw their way out of the pot when first dumped in. I guess I would too!

St. Marks River Cabin

My step-father and mother greeting friends to the cabin

My family had one of the few cabins ever located up the St. Marks River. My father leased the land from a local man and he and some of his friends built the cabin in the mid 1950s. On weekends, we went to the Newport bridge boat ramp off highway 98 and launched our boat to travel upriver to the cabin. Later the St. Joe Paper Company cut a logging road in the woods behind the cabin and we'd take our four wheel drive jeep up the road then drive a half mile through the woods to the cabin.

It had a wide screened in front porch with wicker rocking chairs where you could sit and watch the river. Inside, there was an open room that contained a kitchen equipped with a gas stove and a sink over which perched a tulip handle water pump. There was also a rough hewed wooden table with benches. On the other side of the room were two double beds. Outside, behind the cabin, was a two-seater outhouse. We used to go to the outhouse in pairs, one would "go" and the other would look out for snakes.

When my father wanted to spend some alone time with my mom, he would suggest we go pick violets, promising a penny for each one returned. We'd roam the woods for a couple of hours trying to find them and only later figured out that they only grew a certain time of the year. He was a sly one, my father.

Palm Sunday

A large palm tree curved out over the river from the bank in front of our St. Marks river cabin. My sisters and I used to try to run up and down the tree without falling in the water. We were never successful.

One Sunday my father decided to show us how it was done. Before he attempted it, my mother begged him to take off his watch, just in case he fell. He was very cocky and told her not to worry—but he did eventually give her the watch to hold. He stood at the base of the palm and then to our amazement ran to the top and back again in a flash! Seeing our gaping mouths he told us there was nothing to it, all it took was a little coordination, which he had. He then ran up the tree again, but this time he slipped and wound up holding on with his arms and legs wrapped around the trunk. We all laughed when he had to let go and splash into the river, just like we had done so many times. He waded out of the water with a bruised ego, but at least his watch was dry.

The river was a perfect place to catch bream and shell-crackers, as well as a few eels and garfish every now and then. My mother even hooked a squirrel that had the unfortunate luck of being in a tree nearby when she was casting out her line. She used to bring her fishing pole way back over her head then quickly move it forward to cast the line. Imagine her and the squirrel's surprise when she hooked his fur and slung him off his branch into the river with a loud splash! I never knew squirrels could swim until that day.

Sponges and Ice Cream

My father used to take me down the river to the town of St. Marks to see the sponge boats come into port. The old wooden vessels were piloted by large Greek men who spoke a language I did not understand. When we got close to their boats the pungent smell of the live sponges, strung up to dry on lines which ran from bow to stern, would take my breath away. We looked over the sponges and the crew told us the names of the different types such as sheep's wool, yellow and grass sponges. Each had a different quality and use. We always bought the sheep's wool which was good for washing the car.

On the way back to our cabin my father would point to three large white tanks on the river bank and tell me they were full of ice cream, one vanilla, one chocolate and the other strawberry. I always wanted to get a spoon and check them out. It was years later when I learned they were oil tanks built to store oil brought in by barges from the gulf.

River-Rats

We took boat rides up the St. Marks River and especially liked to go up to an island that had a tent made of tin built on it. Two of the local "river rats" Spud and Jellybean lived in it off and on. They had fashioned it from tin roofing, hub caps and anything else they managed to get their hands on to weld together.

Spud was a jack of all trades and hired himself out to earn money to pay for beer and food. Jellybean was Spud's best friend. The son of a well-to-do family, Jellybean was born and raised in Wakulla County. His initials were J.B which may be the reason everyone always called him Jellybean. He had gotten into trouble running with the wrong crowd as a teenager and had decided to drop out of life long before he ever dropped in. In spite of his troubles, he was a gentle soul with a good disposition. It was really hard to ever make him mad, he'd just grin and say "Think nothing of it", whenever something happened. Local folks used to say that Jellybean's father was "sharp as a tack" but when it came to him "the needle was a little dull."

Though we were never around Jellybean very much Spud often spoke of him. When we first met Spud he was kind of anti-social but through the years he grew to tolerate us, even telling us a few of his stories.

Buzz Cut

One of our river friends, an old "river rat" named Spud, used to stop by and tell us stories about his life on the river. One story involved a "hippie" he had encountered at the original Outz's Oyster Bar in Newport. The young man was dressed in beads and worn jeans as was the counter-culture style of the sixties. He had long flowing hair. He was probably not a hippie from "San- Fran-Sissy-Co" as Spud said, but a student from Florida State University in Tallahassee.

The hippie sat at a table next to Spud and for some reason he decided to pick on Spud and his friend Jellybean as they sat there drinking beer. Jellybean just ignored him but he soon got under Spud's skin. He had let him go on for a while but soon tired of the insults. Without saying a word Spud got up and slowly walked over to the boy and with one quick punch he knocked him out cold!

The boy lay sprawled on the floor unconscious. Spud, not wanting to waste an opportunity, went outside and got his tin cutting shears from his boat and gave him a hair-cut. When he awoke he found Spud and Jellybean gone and a pile of his hair beside him. His head was bleeding from the close cut of the shears. The boy picked himself up and left, never to venture that way again. Spud never said anything else to us about that incident but I have always remembered it—I guess that young "hippie" does also.

Is Slud a word?

Spud told us about a time he helped roof a house with new tin. It can get hot on a tin roof (so Tennessee Williams tells me) and the pieces of tin sometimes are hard to pull across the roof to nail in place. Spud told us he had solved that problem by "Just putting motor oil on the tin and sludding it into place." Imagine what his foreman thought when he came back to inspect Spud's work!

How to Cook a Gar

Spud once told us he had figured out the best way to cook a gar fish.[56] Gar is actually short for alligator gar, named after its appearance with a long toothy mouth like an alligator. When we caught a gar we always tried to get it off the hook and back into the water instead of our boat. Gars are scavenger fish that feed off the bottom, eating anything that happens to lie there. The meat is white, but smelly so no one would ever eat it. We were especially interested to hear of Spud's recipe as we had never heard of anyone who had actually cooked and eaten gar.

Spud started by saying, "First you need to dig a deep pit. Then you lay a bunch of palmetto fronds down in a pile. On top of the palmetto you add a layer of cow

---

[56] The Alligator Gar is a freshwater fish with a long snout that displays its alligator-like teeth. Bow-hunters like to hunt them as they tend to float near the surface making them easy prey. Some people even eat them!

manure." We eyed him with a little doubt when he mentioned that last ingredient but he looked at us seriously and continued. "Then you keep on layering the palmetto and cow manure until the pit is half full. "

By now we were getting kind of sick thinking of this mixture, but he went on, "You wrap the gar in tin foil and place it in the middle of the pile, then continue filling the pit in the same way as before. When it's full, pour a gallon of kerosene over it and set it on fire, let the fire burn until all that's left are ashes. Then, he said with a smile, Dig out the tin foil with the gar, throw it away and eat the cow manure!"

Jellybean

One night when we were spending the weekend at the river cabin, Spud came to tell us that his friend Jellybean had died the week before. He sat on the front porch and rocked slowly in one of my father's rocking chairs as he remembered his friend.

Spud told us that when Jellybean had turned eighteen his father encouraged him to join the military but he was quickly drummed out of boot camp as unfit for the service. He returned to Wakulla County and spent his days working odd jobs and drinking anything he could buy, beg, borrow or steal.

Jellybean could play the guitar and liked to think of himself as a country singer. Often he'd find him in the woods, drunk and wandering the dirt roads of the county strumming his beat-up guitar and yelling out bits of any songs he could remember.

Spud said he had met Jellybean at a dog fight in Newport one night and they just "hit it off". They decided to build a place where they could get away and drink—so they built a tent made of tin on a small island up the St. Marks River. The two of them would stock up on booze and disappear up the river for a week or so. When they ran out of supplies they'd come back to town to find odd jobs to pay for another round of drinking.

Spud told us that the only other time Jellybean had ever left town besides when he joined the service was when he went to Weeki Wachee Springs to see the mermaids. He fell madly in love with one of the mermaids who worked there and they got married after only a week of dating.

They spent their weekend honeymoon in Tarpon Springs and while there his new wife decided to get a large tattoo of a manatee on her back. When she returned to work on Monday she found that the owners of the attraction were not too pleased to have one of their mermaids so adorned, which effectively ended her brief career as a mermaid. They lived together in her trailer for another month but when her money ran out he did too, leaving matrimony for the Wakulla woods. If she ever followed him back to Wakulla county Spud never mentioned it.

The night Jellybean died he was the victim of a hit and run driver on Highway 98. It was never known definitely if he had been walking or lying down in the road the night he was hit. Spud said his daddy had his body brought back to the house where they dressed him in his only suit, one he had bought from a traveling musician. It had sequins on the shoulders and the outline of a guitar across the front with the name "Eddie' embroidered where the frets went. They laid him out in his casket in their living room. Everyone in town came by to pay their respects to the family, each with a memory of an encounter with Jellybean.

Spud told us that Jellybean was buried in the Crawfordville cemetery. His headstone reads simply "Jellybean, born 1934-died 1966." After the funeral Spud never went up the river again. It's been years since I have been there, but I bet the tin tent is still standing just as I remember, waiting for its occupants to return for one more party.

Bad Company

Spud later fell in with some bad characters from St. Marks. Drug smuggling was rampant in the seventies and in 1978 he was caught driving a semi-truck full of marijuana. A shrimp boat full of marijuana had been pulled into the old Newport ship works to be off-loaded. What Spud and the smugglers did not know was that his truck had been loaded under the watchful eye of law enforcement officers of the multi-county drug task force who were hiding in the rafters of the building.

Agents stopped the truck after it left, seizing it and putting Spud in jail. Spud went to court and argued that he didn't know what was in the truck; he was just trying to make some extra money. The jury wasn't buying his story; consequently he was convicted and sent to prison. I never heard any more about him after that.

Burned out

On June 1, 1967, the 10 year lease on our St Marks river cabin ran out. My father went to see the man he had originally leased it from and found the man had died leaving it to his son who had decided he wanted the cabin for himself. Therefore he refused to renew the lease. He was the type of person who never earned or built anything in his life, always benefitting from the efforts of others. He was not liked very much by the river folks who knew the meaning of a hard day's work. His uppity attitude put them off and they never accepted him like they had his father.

We went to the cabin one last time to clear out our few possessions which included some dishes and silverware, a horseshoe that hung over the entrance, a few deer head mounts and my father's bullwhip that hung beside the door. We left that place with a lot of good memories in our hearts and a longing to spend extra time there to make more.

Two weeks after we had moved out of the cabin it burned to the ground. It was reported as a case of arson probably set by some locals. We had been there 10 years without any problems from the locals but when word got around the river about the arrogant son wanting to use it, the place was destroyed. They even set the outhouse ablaze. A once popular song called *Proud Mary* by Credence Clearwater Revival says that "people on the river are happy to give" but it doesn't mean they were happy to live with people who took things away from others.

Camping Out

We still went to the river to fish and camp after losing the lease on the cabin in 1967. One Labor Day weekend we went upriver with my parent's friends, Hamp and Rae Hutchinson, and their kids, Morgan and Roy. The adults pitched a tent and the kids decided to string up hammocks between the trees to sleep.

It turned out we had picked the rainiest weekend that ever hit the area. In an attempt to make some shelter, we built a lean-to next to an oak tree and covered it with layers of Spanish moss. To our surprise it worked for a while, but soon it failed and we got soaked.

During a lull in the rain, Hamp volunteered to try to re-light the smoldering fire we had made earlier to dry things out and provide some warmth. To help get it going he decided to use some gasoline from the tank supplying his boat motor. We moved a safe distance away while Hamp unhooked the tank from the motor and started to pour some gas on the fire. The gas was mixed with oil so at first it did not do anything but smoke a lot.

Hamp poured on more gas and suddenly the fire jumped up in a fifteen foot flame with a *whoosh*! Our moss-covered lean-to immediately caught fire and burned like a funeral pyre for an Indian warrior. We all ran from the camp trying to get away from the growing fire, each going in a different direction. Hamp back peddled away from the flames still holding the tank which was dribbling a trail of gas on the ground.

To our horror we saw a yellow-blue finger of flame start after him, racing to the tank he was holding. Hamp threw the tank towards the river only seconds before the flames reached it. The tank flew over our boats, landing in the water and blew up, throwing a spurt of fire and water high into the air. A stream of flame danced on the gunwales of the boats while all around the campsite fires flickered.

Hamp's wife, Rae, started screaming at him. While I will not repeat the words she used, it basically questioned his common sense and the fact that he just about killed all of us, in very graphic terms. She was not only upset that he had set the camp and our boats on fire, but that their only gas can, needed to get them back to the boat ramp, had just been destroyed.

After we put the fires out we looked around for anything not wet, singed or smelling like smoke, to get under as the rain began again, this time even harder. It made me think that maybe God had a sense of humor. It had been dry enough for Hamp's episode but then perhaps He started the rain back after having a good laugh!

We had to tow Hamp's family back to the ramp the next day and all the while Rae continued to humiliate Hamp by telling him what a knuckle-headed thing he had done. Personally, I thought it was one of the best nights I had ever spent in the woods. My thoughts changed when I got home and found another surprise — I had one of the worst cases of chigger infestations I had ever seen before or since. I remember standing in front of the bathroom mirror buck naked and seeing that I was literally blood red from neck to ankles with chiggers or "red bugs" as they were called.

If you look up chiggers in a medical book it will state something like "the preferred feeding locations of a chigger are those parts of the body where clothing fits tightly over the skin, such as around the belt line, waistline, and under socks, or where the flesh is tender such as the ankles, armpits, back of the knees, front of the elbow, and the groin." I could have been the poster child for that statement. In terms of feeding on me, let me just say, they had a feast.

My mom filled the tub with alcohol for me to sit in to kill the red bugs and afterwards painstakingly blotted each spot with nail polish to make sure they could no longer breathe. I really doubted the nail polish would work as those things were so imbedded. They probably could hold their breath for hours.

I looked like the walking dead that night, stiffly maneuvering into my bed smelling of rubbing alcohol and covered with blotches of red and pink nail polish (there were so many spots she ran out of the red). To make matters worse I was told not to scratch. Those chiggers and our memorable camping experience that weekend still make me laugh today.

The Newport Sulfur Spring

photo by author

We used to go to an old rundown house that had been built near the spring in Newport. The house had been built during the heyday of the sulfur spring there. In the mid 1800's tourists rode the train from Tallahassee then they'd take a stagecoach to the springs to bathe in the waters and relax. To find the spring today you take Old Plank Road, a dirt road that runs by Outz's Too Oyster Bar. It is located off of highway 98 just before the Newport Bridge. Turn north onto the road and travel about a mile to a small bridge beside the springs. It's obvious there is a sulfur spring nearby because you can smell the strong odor as you get closer.

My only prior experience with sulfur water had been on St. George Island before they put in a water purification plant. It was the only thing we had to drink or to use to brush our teeth. It smelled and tasted like rotten eggs and salt. It was especially terrible when you made ice cubes out of it.

We went to the springs to swim and I remember going to the ruins of the old house and seeing a local man named Jellybean who spent his days drinking, passed out on the floor of that rundown place. The windows had broken shutters that beat against the sides of the building when the wind blew. That coupled with the moaning of that drunken man used to scare the hell out of me.

Spring Creek

Located off the beaten path near Shell Point is a community called Spring Creek. It is named after the boiling underground spring that pumps millions of gallons of fresh water into to the Gulf of Mexico daily. Former Governor Claude Kirk, the first Republican elected governor in 100 years after reconstruction, proposed in 2001 that the spring be capped and used to supply water to help flush the toilets in South Florida which is facing impending water shortages. I doubt if anyone in North Florida is too excited about that idea.

Wakulla Springs

Wakulla Springs, photo by author

Wakulla Springs is one of the four "first magnitude" springs (which means the flow is more than 100 cubic feet of water per second) in the county. The others are Kini, River Sink, and Spring Creek.[57]

The Indians referred to the springs as *Tah-ille-ya-aha-a* which meant "where the water flows upward like the rays of heavenly light out of the shadow of the hill."[58] The waters of Wakulla Springs were called "strange and mysterious waters" by early settlers, probably due to the way the water flows up to the surface then, after running a short distance, disappears again.

Divers have mapped the underground limestone caverns to depths of more than 300 feet and traveled underwater distances of more than 4,300 feet but have yet

---

[57] *"Water Resources Atlas of Florida,"* Edited by Edward A. Fernald and Elizabeth D. Purdum (Tallahassee: Florida State University Institute of Science and Public Affairs, 1998), 57

[58] Frank Drew, "Florida Place-Names of Indian Origin," *Florida Historical Society Quarterly* 6, no.4, (April 1928) :204

to find its source. Based on archeological evidence, early Paleo-Indians lived around the springs. Bones of a mastodon were spotted in the springs in 1850 and removed in 1930. Today they are on display at the Florida Museum of History in Tallahassee.

We used to go to the springs for end of the year school parties and family picnics. The constant 70 degree water temperatures was always enough to refresh anyone trying to cool off on a hot summer day. We'd climb the three tier tower (now only two remain) and dare each other to jump off or we'd take a ride on the glass bottom boats to see Henry.

Henry was called "the pole vaulting fish" but all he really did was swim over a log then the boat operator would drop down fish food to reward him. Because of storm water run-off the waters are not as clear now as they once were and the opportunities to see Henry have been limited to occasional clear days. Boat operators were always entertaining to listen to as they led a guided tour of the river and springs or stopped to call Henry to come pole vault.

On one guided tour when my daughter was in first grade, the operator called everyone's attention to a deer lapping water at the spring's edge. Just as all eyes were focused on the deer, a huge alligator sprang out of the water and grabbed him, pulling the deer into the water and killing it. The children screamed and the flustered boat operator backed the boat away as fast as he could. We finally got the kids calmed down but there was no way we were getting any of them to go swimming that day.

My family was linked to the place by the fact that my parents, who also used to go there as children, spent their honeymoon at the lodge. The Wakulla Springs Lodge was built in 1937 by Ed Ball, executor of the DuPont estate. Ball was a powerful force in Florida's economy and politics, and his legacy is still felt today. He later became the benefactor of Port St. Joe, where the St. Joe Paper Mill was built and run by his company.

The lodge is now run by Florida's Parks and Recreation Division and offers a glimpse of old Florida elegance. Each room has maintained its original look, including 1930 era furniture and bathroom facilities. There is no television in the lodge save for a big screen in the lobby next to the checker board. The restaurant next to the lobby is still a great place to get fried chicken and homemade mashed potatoes, two of their specialties.

There used to be a big black bear in a cage outside the lodge that we'd go see. The cage was small and we felt sorry for him having to be cooped up all the time. He disappeared later; I never knew what happened to him.

No visit to the springs was complete without going to see the remains of "Ole Joe." Joe was an 11 foot alligator that used to hang around the springs. He was shot by unknown poachers in 1966 (a reward still exists for information leading to their arrest). Mr. Ball had him stuffed, mounted in a glass case, and displayed in the lobby of the lodge. Joe is still there today.

Crawfordville

The county seat of Wakulla County, originally in Newport, was moved in 1866 to a new city named in honor of Dr. John L. Crawford.[59] He had served the citizens of the county not only as a doctor, but as a state representative, senator and later as Florida's Secretary of State.

The Crawfordville cemetery is located on the east side of Highway 319 as cars come into town. Every time we passed it my father would ask us if we knew why the people living on the other side of the road could not be

---

[59] Morris, *Florida Place Names*, 60

buried in the cemetery? When we said "We don't know" he'd laugh and say "Because they are not dead yet!"

Jesse and His Gang

When we passed the Wakulla County courthouse my father told us about the time he and some friends were arrested for shooting at road signs. On a weekend home from college, they had taken a boat down to Alligator Point to go water skiing. Later that afternoon, while coming back from the beach, someone had the bright idea to shoot at road signs with a pistol one of them had brought along. As they were also drinking a few beers, it seemed like a great idea.

They traveled up Highway 319 towards Crawfordville shooting at passing signs and mailboxes. It was quickly decided it would work better if a couple of them got in the boat, thereby making it easier to shoot at signs on both sides of the road. This served their purposes well, but their level of excitement was in direct proportion to the amount of beer in their cooler and they soon ran out of both. Motioning to their driver to pull over to the shoulder of the highway, they told him to take them to the nearest bar to restock the cooler.

Their driver stopped at a roadside bar outside Crawfordville. My father climbed out of the boat and went in to buy beer. Unbeknownst to him, one of his friends "Pecker-Face" Woods had also gotten out of the boat and followed him in the bar. I would stop here to explain why he had such a nickname but it's probably better to leave it to the imagination.

Pecker-Face had put the pistol in his belt and as he strolled into the bar he suddenly pulled out the gun and waved it in the air shouting, "Don't a man move nor a woman scream, I'm Jessie James and I'm mean!" The only thing was, he had a hair lip and it came out "Doone aw

53

mawn woove orwa wooman scwame Ima Dwessie Dwames am Ima wean!" the stunned patrons didn't know if they should laugh or be frightened.

My father quickly paid for the beer and hustled "Jessie" out of the bar. It took about five minutes for the local deputy to catch up with "Jessie" and his gang. He arrested my father and his friends and took them to the Wakulla County Courthouse where they all were charged with reckless display of a firearm and put in jail. Getting one phone call, my father called his Uncle Clyde Atkinson, a well known attorney in the area. Clyde was able to convince the Sheriff they were just kids playing a prank and got them released. In court a few weeks later, they each had to pay a $257.00 fine and restitution to the owners of the mailboxes they had shot. Today, every time I drive through that area and see where someone has shot at a road sign or mailbox I think of my father's story.

The Myna

On the outskirts of Crawfordville we'd stop at the old ice plant for a hotdog and a chance to talk to the owner's Myna bird. He was perched in a cage in the middle of the store and would whistle and say "Pretty bird" when a girl walked by, but he'd just look at a boy, feigning indifference to his presence.

The bird's unwillingness to acknowledge me didn't stop me from trying to get him to talk. I'd pepper him with "Polly wants a cracker!" or "Ugly bird!" and he'd hop around on his perch until finally he'd turn his back on me. Then much to my delight he would shout "Damnit!" and other curse words he had undoubtedly heard from his owner or frustrated customers.

Medart

"Me-dart" as we used to call it, sounds like frogs croaking when it's rapidly repeated three times in succession---you just did that didn't you? In Medart we would eagerly look for new Burma Shave signs posted in a field outside of town.

Burma Shave was a men's shaving cream company that started in the 1920s. In an effort to get men who had been used to using a shaving cup and brush to switch to their brushless product, the company started a roadside advertising campaign. It consisted of four to six signs with white lettering on a red background placed one after the other down the roadside, each with a jingle or message and all ending with the company name *Burma Shave*. The signs were placed along the highways all over America from the 30s to the early 60s. The last were erected in 1963, but some survived to entertain traveler's years later. Here's a sampling of some of the sayings on the signs:

On the curves ahead
Remember sonny
That rabbit's foot
Didn't save
The bunny

The Whale
Put Jonah
Down the hatch
But coughed him up
Because he scratched

Her chariot
Raced 80 per
They hauled away
What had
Ben- her

Coastal Highways

It is in Medart that you come to the intersection of
Highway 319 and "The Coastal Highway" (Highway 98).

The road runs the length of Florida's northwest coast
from Pensacola to Perry. At Perry, Highway 98 turns south
and is known as Highway 19/98, winding down to
Chassahowitzka before it turns east to run out at Lake
Worth in Palm Beach County.

Highway 19 continues along the coast until it crosses
Tampa Bay. It then becomes Highway 41 or by the better
known name of Tamiami Trail that turns east in Naples
crossing the Everglades to Miami.

Highway 98 is one of two main coastal highways in
Florida; the other is A1A on the east coast. It was in
traveling these Florida coastal roads that stories of the
Forgotten Coast were written into my soul.

Beach Music

Oyster Radio sign at St George Island Bridge, by author

People going to the forgotten coast nowadays tune in WOYS at 100.5 FM. Called "Oyster Radio" and professing to be "Your beach music connection" the station's format is eclectic at best. You can tune in to a selection of rock and roll, heavy metal, country, easy listening, big band and some songs you will never hear anywhere else (I promise) all in the span of a half hour of listening. A sister channel, devoted entirely to country music, was started on FM 106.5. The station is located in Eastpoint on the road to the St. George Island Bridge.

It was different when I was growing up though. When traveling with my family, we knew when we reached Medart we were close enough to the coast to tune our car radio to AM 138 and listen to some rocking beach music on WLCY from Tampa Bay. We laughed at the stations call signs as the "LC" part sounded like Elsie the Cow, a trademark of Borden's Milk Company.

The DJ's played the latest in rock and roll music and everyone at the beach kept car and portable radios tuned to AM 138. It was as much a part of the beach as the smell of Coppertone sun-tan lotion and the grit of the sand. The station remained a favorite until it went off the air in 1981.

Panacea

Panacea Mineral Springs, photo by author

Formerly known as Smith Springs, the city of Panacea was founded in 1893 by developers. Its name comes from Greek mythology after the goddess of healing, Panacea.[60] It

---

[60] Morris, *Florida Place Names*, 190

was so named because of the supposed healing properties of the mineral springs in the area. [61]

Two hotels, the Panacea Mineral Springs Hotel and the Bay View Inn were built to accommodate early 1900s tourists who came from all around to bathe away ailments in the springs. Some residents balked at the renaming of the area to promote tourism and still refer to it as Kings Bay or Ochlocknee Bay.

The springs were located in a pavilion which housed up to 20 springs, each named with a different medicinal value. Ailing bathers could choose to dip themselves pools displaying signs such as "Liver Trouble," "Headaches," "Stomach Disorders," or "Sore Throat," to ease their woes.[62] The water flowed through cedar stumps into pools where people bathed. Business dropped off in the depression era of the 1930s and never came back. Some pavilions still exist as well as a few pools but the water no longer flows as it did in the past.

---

[61] The Panacea Mineral Springs were originally named Smith Springs but changed to encourage tourists to come bathe in its waters.

[62] James R. Knott, *Tales of Tallahassee Twice Told and Untold*, 1995, 83

Mineral springs pool, Panacea photo by author

Panacea is much the same today as it was 50 years ago. There has been some development but it seems the place has lost more than it has gained. The town has always been a fishing community, occupied by one of the last vestiges of commercial fishermen in Florida. The community prides itself on its self sufficiency and was hard hit by the "Net Ban" in 1995 that killed commercial gill-net fishing and along with it their economy.

Working with the Florida Marine Patrol, I came to better understand the hard life of commercial fishermen. When asked what the hardest part of *my* job was, I often replied "Telling someone they can no longer do something they've being doing all their lives."

It was reaffirmed to me one day by a fisherman reacting to no longer being able to use gill nets to catch mullet. He told me, "My granddaddy done it, my daddy done it, and I am a gonna done it, too!" It was this type spirit and determination that officers of the Florida Marine Patrol were faced with when the net ban laws were first implemented.

The Oaks Restaurant

Oaks Motel sign, photo by author

The Oaks Restaurant in Panacea was well known for its seafood. Owned by the Oaks family, their placemats had a picture of an oak tree with acorns at the bottom, each acorn bearing the name of their children. The other side of the mat had games for kids such as word find and mazes to keep us busy while we waited for our food.

The Oaks had ceramic cracker and butter holders on the tables which were shaped like shrimp boats. The butter was laced with garlic and the crackers were sweet. We always looked forward to those crackers as much as the seafood.

61

The inside of the restaurant was decorated with pecky cypress, a beautiful wood paneling cut from "deadhead" cypress logs. Deadheads were those cypress logs that, when being floated down river, had sunk to the bottom. They remained there for years, serving as homes to boring worms which left distinctive markings in the wood. When the logs were later retrieved and milled they made beautiful (and expensive) paneling.

The restaurant was connected to a gift shop that sold all the tacky gifts one would expect for tourists as well as rafts and water toys for kids. Tourists could also stock up on food and drinks for the beach. The Oaks Motel was located next door where families or fishermen stayed.

Rescue Me?

Years later, when working for the FMP, I went out to look for some fishermen who had come to Panacea and were staying at the Oaks Motel. They were late returning from their fishing trip and their wives, back in Georgia, became concerned that they may have broken down and called the Marine Patrol. As was our practice, before we sent a boat out to search the Gulf for people we checked the boat ramps for their vehicles. Not finding the fishermen's truck and boat trailer at the ramp, we then checked the motel where they were staying. In this instance, as in many others, I found the men "shacked up" in the motel with some women they had met. [63]It always put a damper on their party when a uniformed officer knocked on their motel room door and told them they needed to call their wives.

The Oaks closed in 2000, but the buildings still stand as reminders of good food and good times on the Forgotten

---

[63] Shacked up is a term commonly used for either living together or having illicit sex.

Coast. Another member of the Oaks family opened a restaurant in the late 1960s on the Ochlocknee Bay called "Clayton's." It was there where I took my future wife on our first date after an FSU football game.

"Net Ban"

Panacea was ground zero for the fight against the controversial "Net Ban" amendment passed in November 1994 to limit marine net fishing in near shore coastal waters. Local fishermen had for years depended on the income from gill net fishing and the amendment took direct aim at their livelihood. The fishermen banded together to fight the amendment into a group called Save our Seafood (SOS). This was done in opposition to the anti-netting group called Save Our Sealife (SOS). Vendors sold bumper stickers that proclaimed "Bubba Gump was a Shrimper" to remind people that the mythical figure of the movie screen was just like them.

The amendment was approved by 72% of the 4.1 million voters who went to the polls. The majority of the counties voting against it were the smaller, more sparsely populated ones on the west coast. The law went into effect July 1, 1995. Wakulla county resident, and commercial fisherman, Jonas Porter, became the first person arrested, his intent to challenge the validity of the law. Marine Patrol Officer David Roberts and Captain Donald Smith were the arresting officers.

Fishermen formed local and statewide organizations to raise dollars to hire lawyers and lobbyists to overturn the law. One such organization was the Florida Fishermen's Association located in Panacea which was an outgrowth of the Wakulla Fishermen's Association. It was headed by Ray Pringle. The Association printed newsletters asking for donations and lambasting the law and their perceived treatment by enforcement officers.

In one 1999 newsletter, Pringle's father, a minister and State Chaplin for the Association lambasted the environmental groups and compared the Marine Patrol officers to Nazis, something that certainly did nothing to ease tensions or show a spirit of cooperation. He stated "These greedy, blind environmentalist politicians and bureaucrats care nothing for the poor, the handicapped, and the elderly, who struggle under their oppressive and irresponsible laws and regulations, enforced by the Marine Patrol and the Department of Environmental Protection arbitrarily like Hitler's Nazi Gestapo thugs. These atrocities insult God Almighty and, my beloved fishermen friends; He will visit this sin of injustice upon these villains, politicians, bureaucrats, and officers." [64]

The associations rallied fishermen to hold demonstrations at the state capital, local courthouse grounds, and the Florida Marine Patrol headquarters. Demonstrators dumped dead fish at some locations and others wore vests made of gill netting with fish hung in them to protest the smaller mesh size limits. Fish-fry's were held for sympathetic legislators and supporters. The public was warned that fried mullet dinners, a staple of fund raisers for church socials along the west coast, were in jeopardy.

Attorneys for both the recreational and commercial fishermen challenged every case in court. Trials became as lengthy and detailed as trying a murder case. New rulings concerning how to measure a net, how many nets you could fish at one time and total amount of square footage allowed were passed down from local county judges, upheld or overturned by Circuit judges then reviewed by Supreme Court justices. Every ruling either emboldened or deflated the fishermen's hopes.

---

[64] Rev. Ray Pringle, Sr., "State Chaplin's Message," *Florida Fishermen's Federation Newsletter*, (August-September 1999) : 5

All rulings were appealed by the losing side and defended by the winning ones and only the lawyers got rich. The recreational fishing interests worked just as hard as the fishermen to preserve the new laws even going further to lobby for stricter penalties.

Harmonious relationships that had been fostered through the years between the Florida Marine Patrol (FMP) officers and the fishermen became strained due to the new law.

When they were questioned as to what constituted a legal mesh size for mullet nets, "One inch bar, two inch stretch" became the officer's mantra.[65] Most of the fishermen's frustration and animosity was directed towards the officers as they were the most visible as well as the ones responsible for enforcing the new law. Officers in coastal counties had their car tires slashed and families threatened. The situation became so tense that a group of professional mediators from Florida State University were called in by Governor Lawton Chiles. They facilitated a meeting in Wakulla County to discuss the frustrations of both the fishermen and law enforcement personnel.

Leaders on both sides tried to calm the few hot-heads who were making matters worse. Law enforcement personnel were transferred out of areas to calm tensions in some communities and level-headed fishermen reined in some of their more vocal members.

Ronald Fred Crum emerged as one of the spokesman for the North Florida fishermen but soon others challenged his efforts and relations on all sides broke down. The battle lines, drawn by the pro-recreational lobby and the pro commercial fishing lobby, became set in stone with neither

---

[65] A square mesh of net is measured by the distance between the knots in the square along the horizontal equaling the "bar" measurement. "Stretch" is measured by pulling the mesh diagonally and measuring the distance which should be double the vertical. i.e."1 inch bar 2 inch stretch."

willing to negotiate. The Florida Marine Patrol was left in the middle.

Local newspapers and gossip kept the atmosphere charged with arguments and accusations about the unfairness of the law and its enforcement. Fishermen gathered in coffee shops every morning to discuss ways to appeal the law or find ways around it, either legally or otherwise.

Definitions and interpretations of terms in the law became critical. Any memo issued by the FMP about enforcement practices was debated. If word got out that someone had been caught with an illegal net, a crowd gathered to confront the officers when they came back to the dock.

Wax Job

One "net ban" incident that became a sore point with the locals occurred when a netter was spotted fishing in the bay by a FMP helicopter pilot. The fishermen did not particularly like the agency using a helicopter to spot their nets hidden in the marshes or flying over them when they were trying to fish.

On this particular day we had received a call about an illegal netting operation in Levy Bay. The pilot, who was known to be a little bit of a "cowboy," had landed his helicopter on a local dock to meet an officer to take him out to identify the illegal netter. That in itself was probably not a very good idea as it only drew attention to the aircraft. A patrol boat was dispatched as well. The fisherman was caught in the act of fishing his illegally sized gill net and the officer in the patrol boat brought him back to the dock in Panacea.

The helicopter also returned and landed on the dock. A crowd had gathered and some of the bystanders were buffeted by winds from the helicopters rotor blade as it landed. The arrest was carried out amid the shouts of the fishermen. One of them started complaining that he could no longer hear, claiming the helicopter noise had made him deaf. A call was made to the Tallahassee general headquarters with the man's complaint.

An investigation was initiated and the man hired a lawyer to sue the state for his hearing loss. The issue drug on for a couple of years until it was finally decided to settle the complaint to avoid the cost of a trial. He was given an unspecified sum of cash to drop his lawsuit. While it was thought to be a great victory in the community, some at the agency felt they could have proved his hearing loss was not on account of helicopter noise, but the fact a doctor had noticed that his ears were impacted with ear-wax. He probably had not heard much in quite a while.

Beginning of the End

Monday, May 10, 1999 was a festive day at the Wakulla County Courthouse. Pick-up trucks bearing faded "Save Our Seafood" and "Bubba Gump was a Shrimper!" bumper stickers were parked in front and behind the courthouse.[66] A huge tent was erected on the lawn and a group of men were frying fresh mullet. People formed a line at the tables where they were served cheese grits, coleslaw, hushpuppies and mullet. A yellow igloo water cooler dispensed sweet tea at the end of the line.

Ruddy faced fishermen laughed and talked to each other as local elected officials and dignitaries shook hands with people in the crowd making sure they were seen by the voters. The County commissioners of Wakulla County

---

[66] Save Our Seafood was an organization formed to oppose the controversial net ban in the 1990s. Bubba Gump was the fictional name of a Tom Hanks character in the 1994 movie *Forest Gump* based on a book of the same name by Winston Groom.

had sponsored the fish fry that day in support of their commercial fishermen with all the fish being donated by local dealers. The chairman of the Commission even took a turn frying fish.[67]

They were all there to see that justice be served in the trial of one of their own, a Spring Creek man and his son who had been caught red-handed with an illegal net in the water. All were certain that at the end of the day their friends would walk away free men and the statewide voters, lawmakers, attorneys and enforcers would be proved wrong in their unfair net laws. A high priced attorney stood ready for the defense while a local state attorney handled the case for the State of Florida.

Inside the courthouse at the same time the fish fry was going on, a jury of peers to hear the case was being selected. The judge had warned potential jurors not to accept mullet dinners or have anyone talk to them about the case as it would be considered jury tampering, but it would have been a hard order to enforce that day.

The event leading up to this gathering had all started one October day in 1997. That day Florida Marine Patrol Officer Bubba Joyner was in his new airboat patrolling the waters off Apalachee Bay. The boat had just been rigged and was making one of its first trips into the gulf on patrol. Since the boat was new, the fishermen did not recognize it as a patrol vessel. It was decided to use this fact as an advantage and patrol around the area as an undercover boat. Save for a blue light mounted behind the operator and a siren in front, it looked like any other airboat out on the water. There were a few fishermen that took their chances illegal net fishing and for those that did, this might be a way for the Florida Marine Patrol to get a jump on their activities.

---

[67] "Fish Fry Held While Juries Are Selected," Wakulla News, May 13, 1999.

Officer Joyner had launched his boat at the lighthouse boat ramp in St. Marks and gone out into the bay. He was dressed in civilian clothes to look like a recreational fisherman but he had his gun on his hip and his agency badge prominently displayed beside it.

He rounded Big Pass Island and saw in front of him two men in an airboat fishing a monofilament gill net set in the water. Mullet were jumping in the water inside the net. On the bow of the airboat a young man was slowly pulling in the net and removing mullet. He was in for a surprise this day as the sound of the officer's boat startled him. He turned and saw it coming towards them and immediately dropped the net. His companion ran to the controls of his airboat, fired up the engine and attempted to flee. The officer, his blue lights flashing and the siren blaring easily caught up to his boat and yelled at the operator to stop.

The operator, realizing that his boat was inferior to the officer's new airboat, pulled back on the throttle and let his boat settle in the water. Deciding that while he might be caught he did not have to like it, he became as closed mouth as a clam. Officer Joyner asked him what he had been doing and he said he was only looking at a net they had found in the water.

Officer Joyner knew the two fishermen well; they were a father and son named Leo and Ben Lovel. Joyner told them to return to their net and finish pulling it out of the water but Leo refused to not only help but he also said he did not want the net on his boat since it was not his. His son Ben agreed to come aboard Joyner's boat to help pull in the net. When the net was retrieved the violators were escorted to the boat ramp where more officers met up with Joyner to assist him in picking the fish out of the net. The catch exceeded 300 pounds of mullet.

While they were at the ramp an old man who saw the net boat come in walked over and asked Leo if he could buy some fresh mullet from him. Leo, who had been denying that he owned any of the fish or the net then had the audacity to tell him he would sell him some of his catch.

The sale of the illegally caught fish was nixed by the officers arresting him. Although as he was trying to sell seized evidence, Leo did not like the fact that the officers had told him he could not sell the fish so he sat and fumed. Both Leo and Ben were given citations that listed three charges. They were each cited for fishing with over 500 feet of net, using an illegal type net (gill) and attempting to flee and elude a police officer.

As was customary in such cases, the nets and catch were seized and placed into evidence. The fish were later sold for the highest market price found with the proceeds being put in an escrow account until settlement of the case by a judge. The net was stored at the Marine Patrol office in Carrabelle until trial.

On Monday May 17, 1999, a week after the fish fry, it was Leo and Ben who were in the frying pan. The case was presented before a jury who first heard the arresting officer's testimony and then it was time for the defense.

Taking the stand, Leo proceeded to "melt down" under the prosecutions questioning in a scene reminiscent of Colonel Jessup in the movie "A Few Good Men." After his performance, his defense attorney probably wished he had made a plea bargain, but it was too late. Both Leo and Ben were found guilty by the jury. The jury had found them innocent of fishing with a gill net and resisting arrest by attempting to flee, but both were adjudicated guilty on one count each of tying two 500 square foot nets together to make a larger single net.[68] The Judge ordered both to pay a $225.00 fine and to forfeit their fishing gear and money from the catch. Because it was considered a major violation

---

[68] "Crum Acquitted, Lovel's Convicted," Wakulla News, May 20, 1999

of the net fishing laws, both were also subject to civil penalties. The state suspended their commercial fishing licenses and privileges for three months and each had to pay a $2,500 fine. Added to these fines was a hefty lawyer's fee making the cost for those 300 pounds of mullet to far exceed the $1.10 a pound they would have brought at market.

The day of the trial had started as a festive affair around the courthouse but things ended on a more somber note. Leo and his son Ben had been found guilty of a net violation in Wakulla County. The net ban opponents had lost a major battle in the heart of their rural north Florida base. In doing so they had also upheld the state's interpretation of the net ban laws.

It took the wind out of the commercial fishermen's' sails as they now could no longer be sure if they would win or lose when they went to court no matter how many free meals might be served outside the courthouse. Many fishermen decided the battle was lost that day — thanks to Leo and Ben Lovel. Florida's "Net Ban" law had been upheld and the guilty verdict of those two fishermen had changed a way of life forever.[69] Only years later when Leo wrote his account of his arrest did he admit he owned the net.

---

[69] "Net Ban" was the abbreviated term given by the fishermen to the constitutional amendment to limit gill and other entangling nets as well as nets over 500 square feet in nearshore and inshore salt waters.

Fried Mullet

2 pounds of fresh fish
2/3 cup cornmeal*
½ teaspoon salt
½ teaspoon paprika
Oil for frying
Makes 6 servings

Cut fillets into serving size portions. Combine cornmeal, salt and paprika. Turn fish in cornmeal mixture. (I prefer putting all in either a paper bag or a plastic bag and shake until fish are covered with meal mixture)

* For finer texture, use 1/3 cup corn meal mixed with 1/3 cup all purpose flour. (Personally, I use Alabama Fine Grind or Hoover's brand, but any available cornmeal will do.)

Place fish in a deep fry basket and cook in hot oil 3 to 4 inches deep at 350 degrees for 2 to 3 minutes; turn fish once when crisp and golden brown. If frying fillets brown the skin side last. Remove from oil and drain on paper towels.

"Shut Your Mouth" Hushpuppies

A staple for any seafood meal, hushpuppies come in many variations, using many different liquids from milk to creamed corn to beer---whatever your preference. You can find hushpuppy recipes on the cornmeal packages used to make batter as well. As folklore would have it, these tasty treats were created by hunters and fishermen from leftover batter and cooked to throw to their dogs to "hush the puppies!"

1 cup cornmeal
1 cup all purpose flour
1 tablespoon baking powder
1 teaspoon sugar
1 teaspoon salt
1/8 teaspoon cayenne pepper
¾ cup milk or buttermilk
2 eggs, beaten
½ cup chopped onion
¼ cup melted margarine or cooking oil
Makes approximately 4 dozen hushpuppies
Sift dry ingredients together. Add remaining ingredients and stir only until well-blended. Place a dollop of approximately 1 tablespoon of batter at a time into the hot oil. Fry until golden brown on both sides. Remove from oil and drain on paper towels. Serve.

Cheese Grits

A true "southern" delicacy, fish just aren't the same without a bowl of "Georgia ice cream" (as some in north Florida have lovingly referred to cheese grits) on the side. You may purchase Quaker® "instant" grits in packets or cook regular grits, following serving size suggestions and cooking direction on the box. Some people prefer grits plain, others with butter, or with cheese. I suggest if adding cheese to grits that you purchase a block of sharp cheddar cheese, grate and mix into grits before serving.

Coleslaw

Coleslaw, along with grits and hushpuppies is another staple of a North Florida fried fish dinner. Slaw may be purchased already prepared at the store or homemade.

Sweet Tea

In North Florida we make our tea sweet enough to put one into a diabetic coma, many a restaurant has been judged unworthy for not having their tea sweet enough.

Pour 2 cups of sugar into a half gallon pitcher
Add ½ gallon boiling hot water
Place 4 family size tea bags in the pitcher (I prefer Luzianne Decaffeinated tea)
Let stand 30 minutes, drain and remove tea bags then stir.
Allow to cool in refrigerator or serve over ice.

Ochlocknee Bay

In the 1950s and 60s the sale of liquor, either by the drink or bottle, was regulated by local voters, some allowed one or both, some neither. This created a patchwork of "wet" counties that allowed the sale of liquor, and "dry" counties that did not, in Florida.

Five dry counties still exist in Florida today, and many areas still have "blue laws" that prohibit alcohol sales on Sunday. It was only in the winter of 2008 that the city of Port St. Joe agreed to allow the sale of alcohol on Sundays.

Leon County had been both over the years. During the dry periods in Tallahassee "bootleggers"[70] came to town from neighboring counties to sell liquor to any in need. I remember my father had two bootleggers, one named Smitty and the other Jake. Both drove Cadillac's and made weekly runs to town, their trunks loaded down with various types of liquor from scotch to bourbon and gin. They would even come to the house to fill client's orders.

At the coast, an enterprising businessman had built a bar and package store out over the Ochlocknee River called the Bridge Café and Bar, it was located next to the Highway 98 Bridge which separated the two counties. The river was considered the dividing line between the two counties. Wakulla County was "dry" in the sense that you could not buy liquor by the bottle or drink, but you could bring your own bottle (BYOB) and drink at their restaurants. Neighboring Franklin County was "wet", allowing liquor sales by the bottle.

To get to the bar you would park on the Wakulla County shore and walk out on a dock to the building on

---

[70] The word bootlegger comes from the Midwest in the 1880s to denote the practice of concealing flasks of illicit liquor in boot tops when going to trade with Indians

pilings in the river thereby entering Franklin County where liquor sales were legal.

On the north side of the bridge, also built over the water, was a place called Georges Café and Bar owned by the Petrandis family. They also built a hotel called Georges on the shore side property. The bar was leased to Ken and Alice Faiver in the late 1950s who converted it into a seafood restaurant called Faivers. Patrons would go to the bar across the road and purchase a bottle of liquor, then go to Faivers where they would get "set ups" (ice and cola) to have with a seafood meal.

The restaurant still exists though rebuilt and named after one of George Petrandis's sons who now runs it. The liquor store/bar on the other side of the bridge is gone, replaced by a campground.

Packages

When we traveled to the coast, the way we went depended on how early we left, or if my father needed to go to the "package store," after we turned onto Highway 98. If he needed to pick up a "package" we stayed on the coastal highway through Panacea and Ochlocknee Bay, Alligator Point and St. Teresa. If we did not need to stop for a package we would take a spur off the highway onto the Sopchoppy Highway (319), which went through Buckhorn and the city of Sopchoppy. Both roads meet again a few miles outside of Lanark Village.

Being young, I really thought my father was stopping to pick up presents for us when he stopped at the "package store," never realizing until I got older that it was a liquor store.

After my father had loaded up with enough booze to get him through a weekend of kids at the beach we'd continue, passing through Alligator Point and St. Teresa. Sometimes we stopped at the store at Wilson's Beach, then

we'd go on to Turkey Point where the Sopchoppy
Highway would meet Highway 98 again.

Sopchoppy

The name Sopchoppy is said to come from the Creek
Indian language. Two words, "sokhe" and "chapke" were
combined, together they mean "twisted" and" long".[71] The
town got its name from the river, undoubtedly so named
by the Indians to describe its flow. Others say the name
comes from a Muskogee word "lokchapi" which means
the red oak, the "lokcha" meaning acorn and "api"
meaning stem.[72]

The town was surveyed in 1895 by John Calhoun
Hodge, called the founder of Sopchoppy, when he was
working for the Scottish Land and Improvement
Company. The Georgia, Florida and Alabama railroad
passed through the town in 1893, bringing transportation
and commerce to the area. In the early 1900s the town
supported thriving lumber, farming, and tupelo honey
businesses. Before adequate roads were built, tourists
would come by train to Sopchoppy, and then take a tram
to the Panacea mineral springs and hotels.

Sugar Daddies

We would often stop on the outskirts of Sopchoppy at
the Standard Oil filling station. There we'd buy Orange
Crush, Nu-grape, Dr. Pepper or RC Cola sodas, plus some
kind of treat to eat. I especially liked to get a "Boxcar",
delicious packages of gingerbread crackers with red

---

[71] Simpson, *A Provisional Gazetteer of Florida Place-Names of Indian
Derivation*, 99
[72] Morris, *Florida Place Names*, 224

frosting, or a Sugar Daddy, a hard caramel sucker on a stick.

When we got Sugar Daddies, my sisters and I would challenge each other to see who could make theirs last the longest. In retrospect, it was probably my father who thought up the game as a way to keep us quiet as we traveled.

Grunting Worms

Grunting worms is an art that has been passed down from generation to generation. It consists of driving a three foot homemade wooden stake, called a "stob", into damp or wet ground and then rubbing an "iron", a 4 inch by 2 foot piece of heavy iron, across the top of it. When done properly this creates a low, guttural, grunting noise and causes the ground to vibrate. It is said to recreate the same effect a digging mole, seeking worms for dinner, has on the ground. Nonetheless, it excites the worms, driving them to the surface where they can be picked up and then sold for fishing bait. "Baiting" worms (as it is called by the locals) has also been called "grunting,""rooting, "worm charming," or "fiddling worms."

Located on the outskirts of Sopchoppy is a predominately black community called Buckhorn whose residents make their living fishing, pulp-wooding, and baiting worms. Many a local family still survives on the bait business, sometimes making as much as $300.00 a day. A friend and former co-worker, Antonio Kilpatrick, had grown up in Buckhorn baiting worms and agreed to show me how it was done. I met with him one cold January morning to go out and learn this lost art.

I picked Antonio up at the Expressway in Sopchoppy where he loaded his "stob", bait can, and a flat piece of iron into the back of my truck. Because it was hunting season, he also took along his rifle in case we saw deer.

We drove into the flat woods of the Apalachicola National Forest, turning down graded dirt roads that bore fresh signs of deer hooves, looking for a good clearing to start. Antonio explained that newly burned off parcels of land were best to see the worms when they rise, but he cautioned that it was better to go there after a rain as the worms tend to die from the potash residue if harvested before a rain had washed it away. He scanned the woods and finally said to stop at a cleared patch of forest with only a light amount of palmetto bush and grass covering the ground.

Walking into the woods we noticed signs of a recent visitor to the area, a black bear that had been eating palmetto berries, evidenced by his droppings. Antonio said the land looked good, not too wet or too dry. Worms tend to like moist ground and when the ground is too wet they will move towards dryer ground and vice versa when the land is too dry.

Using the heavy iron, he pounded his stob into the ground. I asked him how he knew how far to go and he said when it "felt right", about a foot and a half was my best estimate. He told me the stob would sink further into the ground as you ran the iron across it, sometimes almost sinking to its hilt in really moist ground. He stooped over the stob and began to move the iron across its top from left to right. He said most people do it the other way but this was the way he had felt most comfortable doing it through the years. As the iron moved in his hands it made a short noise that sounded like a guttural moaning and I could feel the ground vibrating in waves that emanated from the center of the partially buried stob to about 20 feet all around it. Each pass of the iron resulted in the same effect as Antonio methodically went through the motions that he had done for a lifetime. He called the motions "bumping" or "scratching". He'd go through a series of five or six then look around the area for worms.

After about five minutes he rose and started walking around the immediate vicinity of the stob, picking up earthworms. You could see them coming up through the soil to the top of the grass: long, thick earthworms, first one or two, then more and more. A baiter will count their worms as they pick them up figuring about 500 worms to a can. On a good day, where you may start at 4 in the morning and bait until about 9 or 10 o'clock, you can get 4 to 5 cans. The worms are then brought back to town and sold to the local bait shops. The bait shop separates the worms into cups of 24 worms apiece to be sold.

Antonio told me that when baiting you have to "follow the worms" as you go, noticing where your heaviest concentration is and moving towards that area with your stob and iron after each try. After working an area he would hit the side of the stob with the iron to loosen it from the ground then walk to another area and try again.

After watching Antonio try in a couple of places with much success, I asked if I could have a go at it. He showed me how to hold the iron and instructed the motion I should try to make. At first I was clumsy, not getting much of a sound and the iron seemed to drag over the stob. He told me not to try so hard and just move it in a rhythmic motion across the stob then lift the iron and bring it back to start again. Slowly I got the hang of it and it dawned on me how peaceful and sweet the sound of the music was that the iron made. I became more relaxed listening to the sounds and moving my arms to its rhythms. "Look" said Antonio, "here come the worms!" And sure enough I had been rewarded for my brief efforts with dozens of shiny earthworms. Time to go fishing?

In the late 1960s, Charles Kuralt, a CBS television reporter, started a show called "On the Road with Charles Kuralt" that showcased small town America and her people. He was drawn to the Sopchoppy/Buckhorn area after hearing about locals that were baiting worms and came to show the world the unusual practice.

While Kuralt publicized the town of Sopchoppy and worm grunting, it was a little bittersweet for the locals. After seeing people making a living baiting in the National forest, the U.S Department of Agriculture's Forest Service started requiring a Bait Harvesting Permit (called a "bait sticker" by the locals) at the cost of $58.00 a year. Many thought that the Forest Service was trying to figure out a way to make money off the people, but in reality, it was a preservation concern. When baiters went into the woods hunting good ground for baiting, many would just burn off an area thereby making it easier to see the worms rise. Needless to say there were more than a few fires that got out of hand, costing the Forest Service time, money and manpower to control. If you ever get down to Sopchoppy in April, go to the Worm Grunting Festival and Ball, try your hand at baiting, dance a little – and get yourself a tee-shirt to prove you did.

Smith Creek

As you drive through the city of Sopchoppy heading west, you'll see that the road changes its name to Smith Creek Road when you get out of town. In the early 70s my father, wanting to have another river place to get away to, bought a piece of land in Smith Creek near Jack Langston's Fish Camp. The property fronted on the Ochlocknee River. My father named the road leading into our place "Easy Street." He said he had always wanted to live on easy street , that mythical place where one had no bills and no worries. Years later, when the county started maintaining the roads in the area, the street was officially named Easy Street due to my father's efforts.

We cleared the lot enough so we could see the river and had a two bedroom single wide trailer placed there.

My father always had an attraction to pictures of chimpanzees dressed up like humans and I remember he had a bunch of them framed and mounted that hung along the walls of the trailer hallway. Later we added another bedroom and a separate concrete block building with a fireplace and game room downstairs, and an up-stairs screened- in porch where we could cook out and sit on rocking chairs while watching the river.

My friends and I built a deck with stairs leading down to a floating dock on the river. My father had a friend build him a concrete fish pool with a fountain surrounded by limestone rocks. He placed a sign near the pool that read, "We don't swim in your toilet, so please don't pee in our pool." We would put our smaller bream and catfish in the pool when we returned from fishing. Later our children fished for them in the pool.

We used to sit on our porch and shoot at bottles and paper targets that we'd placed on the bank across the river. In constructing the porch, we had built in a screen framed "window" with a ledge where we could rest the rifle to steady our aim. Most of the time we could shoot with abandon, it was only when the river became busy on the weekends that we would stop. The river house was a place where my family spent many special weekends. As a matter of fact, I spent the first week of my honeymoon there. After my father died in 1986 we sold the place to a friend of mine who kept it for many years.

"Frog gigging"

I spent many nights "frog gigging" on the Ochlocknee River. We'd usually go with three people in the boat: one to operate the motor, one to shine the light, and another to gig. We had an airport runway light which we used to shine the eyes of the frogs and it really lit up the river at night.

The light made their eyes shine and we'd maneuver towards that spot, but many times we'd run up on an alligator instead of a frog! When we did find a frog, the operator would speed the boat towards the bank while the one with the light held it steady on the frog. The designated "gigger" would impale the frog on a four-pronged gig attached to the end of a 10 foot pole, and then swing it into the boat. He had to strike fast before the frog jumped into the water. If his aim was true he was awarded with a big bull-frog. We repeated this process throughout the night until we caught all we needed. It was the legs we were after. Frog legs are considered a delicacy in North Florida and when deep fried, many say they taste just like chicken. It always struck me how the legs would quiver and contract when dropped in the hot grease.

Float Hunting

The Apalachicola National Wildlife Refuge was located across the river from our trailer and we considered it a hunter's paradise. We'd "float hunt", drifting down the river in our boat, shooting squirrels. Sometimes we'd catch a deer swimming across the river. The object of "float hunting" is to be able to come upon the game silently without being noticed. Obviously you can't float upstream so you need an outboard motor or "kicker" as we called it, to get back to camp.

A friend of mine used to swear that the squirrels in those trees were the toughest he had ever seen. He said he once saw one doing push-ups on a tree branch. They were hardy little animals, and they'd sit there and chide you while you were taking aim. We would kill a few then go back to the trailer and cook up a squirrel purlieu (squirrel with rice).

Bush Hooks

If we were not fishing or frog gigging, we'd set out bush hooks for channel catfish. A line was rigged with a hook and baited, then tied to a sturdy bush or tree limb over the river. We'd mark the limb with a piece of colored cloth so we could find it easily.

After placing about 15 to 25 bush-hooks we'd leave, then we'd return later in the evening to check them. You could tell if a fish (or turtle) was on the line as the limb would be dipping or the bush would be moving back and forth. We'd take any fish we caught off and re-bait the hook. We fished the lines the entire time we were at the river. A channel catfish can grow to the size of a small infant and many a time we'd catch one on every hook. We always tried to be responsible about our bush hooks, taking them all in before we left, but many careless fishermen did not.

Although it later became illegal to do so, we used to trap turtles in a wire basket. You'd place the basket under a log on the side away from where you'd normally approach the log from the river. The logic was that the turtle would fall off the log on the side away from the on-coming boat traffic and land in the basket. Usually we caught big alligator snapping turtles and striped head cooters.[73]

Hog Hunting

We also used to hunt "Piney Woods Rooters", short, stocky, feral hogs with long stringy black hair that roamed the pine woods. The pigs are said to be descendents of those brought by Hernando de Soto, a Spanish explorer.

---

[73] Florida Cooters are turtles ranging from 9 to 13 inches, their shells have concentric rings and their head and neck is striped.

He planned to use them as food for his men, but some had escaped into the pine woods during his expeditions in the 1500s. They were the wildest animals I had ever seen. A boar would just as soon attack you as look at you if you came close. If one was ever backed into a corner, he would fight like a whirlwind, afraid of nothing, not even a black bear.

For years and years, farmers had turned their domestic pigs out into the woods to forage on what they called their "hog claims". The claim consisted of tracts of land in the national forest leased by the farmer for his hogs. The domestic hogs had roamed the woods and inbred with the wild piney woods hogs for so long that soon the woods were literally filled with them.

Because the hogs were territorial, they would stay in the general vicinity of where they were released. Once a year the hogs would be rounded up and marked or branded. Some farmers would use "catch dogs" to either grab or hold the hog by the ear or herd it into a hog pen set up in the woods. The dogs were usually curs but soon farmers started breeding them and betting on their prize dog against other farmers dogs in dog fights. You could hunt in these forests, but could not kill any hogs. To do so would result in penalties worse than fooling around with another man's wife.

Usually, farmers posted signs advising hunters of the boundaries of his hog claim and warning of the dire consequences if he killed one of his hogs. In the 1950s all hog claims were rescinded and farmers were given an allotted amount of time to round up their hogs.

Because of their protected status, the hogs did not fear people as long as they didn't get too close. While most domestic hogs were eventually rounded up, a lot of the wily ones that had escaped branding still roamed the woods inbreeding with the piney woods rooters. You could find their telltale signs everywhere, torn up ground where they had dug up roots and young pine saplings. This was another reason they were losing their protected status. Because they especially liked pine tree roots and bark (which tended to give their meat a turpentine flavor), the slash pine and pulpwood companies had cancelled the farmers leases and subsequently the hogs protected status. Companies did not like them eating their profits and upsetting the environment, considering them as one would the plague.

In the early 1970s, with the beginning of the fall hunting season, hogs officially became fair game, and in Wakulla County it was like shooting ducks in a barrel. We went out that December hunting for hogs for a New Years day cook-out. After a short walk in the woods, we found a big old sow with two young shoats. We did not want to kill a boar as they were too gamey and the meat was tough.

My hunting partner, Greg Thigpen, set his sights on the sow and I took the two shoats. As soon as they realized we were getting near they started running, but for some strange reason they ran in a large circle around us. Standing back to back and moving with the hogs, we'd draw a bead on one and shoot and it would fall squealing to the ground, while the other two kept running. After we killed all three, we nailed them up to trees by their hind legs and field dressed them.

When we got home, we dug a deep pit in the backyard and started a huge fire of hickory logs. We continued to stoke the fire for about six hours. When the fire had burned down to a large bed of hot embers, we put the pigs on the grill for another six hours, slow-cooking the meat. We fed about thirty people from those three hogs and it was some of the best pork I ever had.

Lake Hitchcock

Lake Hitchcock is a beautiful lake situated off the Ochlocknee River. There are large cypress, oak, magnolia, sweet gum and tupelo trees all around the lake. The bottom of the lake has many sandy areas which were great for "bedding up" fish in the spring.

To make the fish get on the bed, we'd usually go out a few days before a full moon and start preparing our spot. We looked for an area near the bank that had some shade overhanging the river. There we'd spread about 25 pounds of soybean meal (bought at a feed store in 100 pound bags) over the spot. We'd not fish it for two days, instead each evening we'd return to spread the same amount of soybean meal at the time we wanted to fish. On the third day we'd go back and spread a large bowl of soybean meal over the same area, then we started fishing.

It took about a minute for the fish to begin to bite. We'd catch 50 to 100 every time. These were not small fish either, but the big studs that wanted to be first over the bedding females. When caught, they were so big you had to hold them firmly to your chest to remove the hook. So we called them "titty bream". Only thing was you had to be careful as they had a way of peeing on you when they were held up close, probably on purpose for hooking them.

This particular trip, fishing was not on our mind — hunting was. One morning, three friends and I left our trailer on Easy street to hunt in the Lake Hitchcock area. We planned to go all the way around the lake searching for squirrels, hogs or deer. The boat was small, only 14 feet long, so one person sat on the bow, two in the middle seat and I was at the stern operating the motor.

We had decided to break up into two two-man teams, so I dropped one team off at a predetermined spot. Bill and I went a little further around the lake to a place I knew was full of squirrels and where I had seen hog signs the day before. We ran the boat up on the lake shore and tied it off to a sweet gum tree.

Both of us scouted the area but did not see any fresh signs of any hogs so we decided to squirrel-hunt. But we had a problem. We had filled our vests with shells to shoot hogs, not squirrels. I had 10 low brass eights so we decided to hunt with those and get what we could before running out of ammunition. We had shot about five squirrels when Bill noticed something high up in a sweet-gum tree. It was hard to see what it was but Bill saw some movement and decided to shoot. He hit the animal and it fell out of the tree, dead as a doornail, landing near our feet with a loud thump.

I went over to look and saw it was a raccoon—totally worthless to eat as far as I was concerned. We had a rule against shooting anything we were not going to eat, so I got kind of mad at Bill. To make matters worse, it was a mother raccoon with seven young clutching to her when she fell. The blind, dazed baby raccoons were running around our feet and squealing for their mother. Because we did not have enough shells to shoot them all, I picked up a tree limb and started killing them. Bill must have thought I had gone crazy as I ran around crushing their skulls with the limb, but I knew they could not survive without their mother. At the time there were no such things as wildlife rehabilitation centers which could have saved them.

After they were dead, we got back into the boat, not saying much to each other, Bill, because he was a little squeamish about the prior ordeal, and I because I was mad that it had to have been done in the first place. I picked up the other two hunters and started back to our camp. They noticed we were quiet and instead of saying anything, kept to themselves.

When we were about a quarter of a mile from the camp our motor stopped running. I tried to restart it but had no luck. We were coming upriver so if we did not hold on to the shrubs on the bank, we would start going down river again. Because paddling was not an option, we decided to pull our boat along the overgrown banks by the overhanging branches.

Bill, the mama raccoon killer, started complaining about how hard it was and decided not to help pull us along anymore. By then I had pretty well had enough of him, and if he had been sitting closer, I probably would have thrown him overboard, instead I just glared at him. Later my other friends said that if looks could have killed, Bill would have been stone cold dead. We finally made it back to camp and the next day we left. That was the last time I ever went hunting with Bill.

The days I spent on Easy Street call to me in my memories and come rushing back whenever I walk in the woods on a crisp fall day or float down a river. When I see where piney woods rooters have torn up the earth or watch a raccoon skittering away from a river bank I think of days hunting and fishing with my friends.

CHAPTER FOUR – FRANKLIN COUNTY

ALLIGATOR POINT TO CARRABELLE

Alligator Point

Alligator Point supposedly got its name from its shape.[74] If viewed from the air it looks like the outline of an alligator. It's possible that Spanish explorers may have named it as well. Many places where they originally landed are named for alligators. I imagine they had some encounters with the prehistoric animals and decided to name the places such to warn future explorers.

Before Alligator Point was developed in the seventies and eighties, it consisted of a small community of beach houses and a way-side park on the beach. A marina, on the west end of the point, is a popular launch site to fish the bountiful waters for trout, redfish and Spanish mackerel.

When I was young, my family spent many summer days visiting families who owned homes there, picnicking and playing at the road-side park. I remember pretending to be the "Flying Wallendas" and performing great feats of skill and acrobatics on the beach.[75]

---

[74] Morris, *Florida Place Names*, 5
[75] The Wallendas were a famous family troupe of circus actors know for daring feats on a tightrope without a net.

St. Teresa

St. Teresa was named after Teresa Hopkins, the only surviving daughter of Arvah Hopkins. He and General Patrick Houstoun, Governor W. P. Bloxham, John Williams and Leroy Ball are credited with starting the beachside colony in 1873.[76] The St. part of the name was not in the original name but was added later for some unknown reason. Maybe some late coming Spanish explorer decided to claim it and rename it.

Old St. Teresa beach area covers a two mile stretch between Grassy Point (near the location of the former Lutheran Church's Camp Weed- now called *Bay North*) and Stingree Point which is just east of the former Wilson Beach store and cottages. Westward from there are Cochran-Phillips Beach and Perkins Beach.

Today the area west of old St. Teresa is slated to become the St. Joe Companies newest development called Summer

---

[76] Randal Hopkins, *Teresa Was Earliest Vacation Spot For Residents After Civil War*, Tallahassee *Democrat*, June 27, 1965

Camp. Initial plans call for 500 home sites with prices ranging from $99,000 to $500,000 with more to come later. Development plans have been slowed by the recent economy but the day will soon come when the area will be as populated as Destin and this part of the forgotten coast will be gone.

St. Teresa was the closest access to the beach for residents of Tallahassee and many of her old time families had cottages there or visited during the summer. If you did not have a place there families could either rough it and camp out, or rent one of the Wilson's cottages. They were small two bedroom affairs with a kitchen and bath and were located close to the beach and fishing pier.

Sandy Feet

My Uncle George Atkinson owned a house at St. Teresa that we used to visit in the summer. It was a simple place with a screened porch and linoleum floors but my uncle was proud of it. He was particular about us kids tracking sand into the house and to keep it down, he placed a wash tub of water outside the door. We were supposed to step in the water to wash the sand off our feet before coming in, and if we forgot, he charged us a penny fine.

My step-brother, Ricky Atkinson, was one of the worst offenders, but considering he was only four you would think it would have been excusable. Not so with my Uncle George. He had a stern look about him and you could never tell if he was serious or not when he spoke to us.

One day Ricky came in the house without washing his feet and my uncle, who was sitting in a rocker on the porch, called him over to him. Looking sternly down at the boy, he asked, "Don't you know you are supposed to wash the sand off your feet before coming in the house?" Ricky shyly nodded his head as my uncle continued, "and don't you know that it will cost you a cent for forgetting?' Once again Rick nodded his head but then he looked up at Uncle George with tears in his eyes and blurted out, "But I ain't got no cents!" My uncles laughter let him know that he was free to go but what he said lived on, and we always reminded Ricky of his lack of sense/cents should he start to get smart with us.

Drip Castles

My cousin Betty Jane Atkinson used to take us with her when she went to her family's beach house for the weekend. She was attending Florida State University and liked to sunbathe on the beach to work on her tan.

One summer she taught us how to make drip castles in the sand. We'd dig a shallow hole with our hands near the shore deep enough to find water, then we'd pull out handfuls of sand dripping with sea water. We'd let it drizzle off our fingers to form sand castles. The sand would pile up in droplets and harden, making intricate designs on the beach.

Being in the first grade at the time, I could probably state with authority that she was the first girl I was ever infatuated with. I loved to be around her and would do anything she asked, even one time agreeing to appear on her sorority float for the FSU homecoming parade.

I was dressed in a referee's uniform and I'd blow my whistle and signal like it was time for play to begin to a bunch of cut-outs painted like Seminole Indians. After the parade was over she gave me a big hug and I felt like I was walking on cloud nine. It was a day I'll never forget.

Big Foot

My father used to take my step-brothers Ricky and Rusty Atkinson and I to my Uncle George's St. Teresa beach house every year for a father-son weekend. He would also invite his best friend Hamp Hutchinson and his son Morgan to join us. We'd spend the weekend fishing, water skiing and playing on the beach.

One of those weekends when I was about eight years old stands out, as it was the time I accidentally got gigged by my friend Morgan. We had gone fishing in our boat and had just anchored it on the sandbar. Then we were walking back through the shallow water to the beach. Morgan had a gig (really just an old broom handle with a nail in it that had the top sharpened) and he decided to try to gig some fish. A group of minnows darted through the water around us and Morgan, thinking he saw a big fish chasing them, slammed the gig down hitting not a fish but my foot. It went completely through my foot between my big and second toe.

At first I didn't know what had happened, but when he pulled it out I felt the pain and saw the blood clouding the water. I started yelling bloody murder. Morgan, believing discretion was the better part of valor dropped the gig and ran like hell towards the beach. With all the blood in the water, I was sure a shark was coming to get me any minute. I started hopping around holding my bloody foot out of the water while my father chased me trying to calm me down. He finally grabbed me and took me to the beach house where he dressed the wound.

All of the boys were upset, thinking I was probably going to lose my foot. My father wasn't much help as he kiddingly told me I could probably get a wooden foot if it had to be amputated. In all the confusion, no one knew where Morgan had gone, and quite frankly, I didn't care. He was later found hiding in a tree behind the house, sitting there quiet as a mouse. I guess he was hoping no one would see him so he could somehow avoid his responsibility for maiming me for life.

Later that night I began to run a fever and had chills. My father became worried and decided to take me back to Tallahassee to get a tetanus shot. I remember the ride back to town lying in the back seat of the car. He stopped at a store on the way and bought me a Sugar Daddy to keep me quiet. I remember sucking on it and looking out the window as we sped to the hospital, wondering what it would be like to have a wooden foot.

After getting the shot, the doctor said I would be OK but would need to stay in town the rest of the weekend. I later told Morgan that I owed him one for gigging me and ruining my weekend. The incident went down in family lore as the day Morgan gigged "Big Foot." Whenever we went fishing afterwards, he would always jump out and run to the beach before I got out of the boat just in case I was planning to pay him back.

Hush Puppies

St. Teresa was a great place to fish and hunt. One winter day, my father, his friend Hamp Hutchinson and I went there to duck hunt. Ducks used to come to the ponds and inland areas of the coast on their migratory flights from the north. Many would land off the beach at St. Teresa. We would drive up to the houses on the beach then peer around them to see if any ducks were in the water out front. If we saw some we'd creep into range and blast away.

It was a cold, bone-chilling day and the air was wet with a foggy mist when we stopped behind a house and I went around front looking for ducks. I saw a group of about thirty and came back and reported it to my dad. We got our shotguns and slowly worked our way down the beach into shooting range, being careful not to scare the ducks away. Soon all three of us opened up with our guns and we killed about six or seven ducks. The dead ducks were floating in a group about 15 yards off the shore. Because of the fog, it was hard to see what kind they were but we thought they were mallards

Since he thought they were mallards, Hamp volunteered to go get them. He stripped down to his underwear and started wading out in the water. The water temperature was probably in the 60s and the outside air was in the 40s so it did not take long for Hamp to lose his enthusiasm about getting the ducks. After retrieving two he stopped and started clutching at his chest. My father became concerned and asked Hamp if he was alright. Then he offered to send me in the water to help him. I don't know where my father got such a great idea, but it sure was nice of him to offer me as a rescuer instead of going himself!

Hamp said he was okay but decided he had enough of the cold water and slowly waded in to shore. His lips and chest had turned blue and he was shivering by the time we got back to the car. He crawled into the back seat and lay down in a fetal position trying to warm up. We piled our jackets on him and my father turned up the car heater full blast but he continued to shake from the cold.

Deciding that Hamp probably needed something warm to drink, we headed back to Panacea to the Oaks Restaurant to buy hot coffee. Hamp stayed in the car while we went in and ordered the coffee and a bag of hushpuppies. Coming back to the car with our goodies, Hamp was able to drink the coffee and eat some of the hushpuppies. Soon he was able to stop shivering enough to get dressed. He ended up with a terrible cold and was sick for a week. Though it has been forty-five years, I can still remember how blue he looked, the strong smell of the coffee, and how good those hushpuppies tasted that day.

Spring Break

Going to St. Teresa was an annual ritual for high school students in Tallahassee. If one had a friend whose family owned a place there they could count on being invited for the week. Usually a group of girls would stay in some of the houses and the guys in others. Then all day and night they tried to find ways to get together out of sight of the watchful eyes of their chaperones. I don't think it has changed much today from when we roamed the beaches looking for a good time.

We were the "*Age of Aquarius*" and "*What a Day for a Daydream*" generation.[77] The revolutionary sixties were going strong but not many were doing drugs and dropping out, that came when some got to college.

John Rudd was (and still is) one of my best friends; his family had bought my uncle's beach house so I still got to go there with him. He and I, plus Jim Foster and Bill Sullivan would go to St Teresa for Spring Break or summer vacation. Jim had a tricked-out dune buggy he would bring that was certain to draw girl's attention. Oftentimes we'd load into the buggy up with our girlfriends and go to St. George Island where we could ride on the beaches or climb the huge sand dunes.

We'd party into the night, walking the beach and coming up on campfires to visit friends or make new ones. If our girlfriends were agreeable, we'd try to sneak off somewhere with them alone.

The beach house was a frequent stopping place when we went to the coast. As we got older, we'd take our dates

---

[77] *Age of Aquarius* was a song from the musical *Hair* and was sung by a group called *The Fifth Dimension* released in 1967. *What a Day for a Daydream* was sung by the *Lovin Spoonful* released in 1966.

there after going to eat at Clayton's or Angelo's.[78] My first date with my future wife ended there, and I think we both figured out we not only liked each other but the beach as well, something that has been a part of our lives ever since.

St James Island

St. James Island is surrounded by three bodies of water: the Ochlocknee and Crooked Rivers to the north and St. George Sound to the south. It encompasses the area from the Ochlocknee River Bridge to where the Crooked River meets the Carrabelle River in Carrabelle. Alligator Point, St. Teresa, Wilson Beach, Turkey Point, Lanark Village and Carrabelle are included on the island.

Regardless of the road we initially took when we went to the coast, highways 319 and 98 meet up just past Turkey Point, a part of the former Camp Gordon Johnson.[79] Our excitement would begin to grow as we passed this landmark, as it was the place where we could actually see the water of the Apalachee Bay.

---

[78] *Clayton's* was a seafood restaurant in Dickerson Bay owned by a member of the Oak's family, the business later burned down. *Angelo's* is still in business, owned by Angelo Petrandis and located at the site of the former Faviers.

[79] Camp Gordon Johnson, originally called Camp Carrabelle, located in Lanark was a World War Two military base used to train troops for the invasion of Normandy on D-Day.

Lanark Village

Old Lanark Village sign, photo by author

The name Lanark comes from the Scottish "Lana" (land) and "ark" (place of refuge). The area has also been known as Lanark-on-the-Gulf and Lanark Springs.[80] It was built by officials of the Georgia-Florida-Alabama railroad in the late 1800's. Originally built as a resort, it boasted a two story hotel, a fenced swimming area in the gulf, and the springs.

In 1942 the land was leased by the United States Army for training soldiers on amphibious landings. The area was called Camp Gordon Johnston after a Medal of Honor winner. It not only served to train troops but also as a prisoner of war camp for Italian and German prisoners.

In 1954 Lanark Estates bought the land and buildings of the camp to create a retirement village. The site of the old officer's quarters is where the village was initially started. In 1957 a developer attempted to enlarge the springs into a lake using a dragline. The limestone outcroppings were

---

[80] Allen Morris, *Florida Place Names*, (Sarasota: Pineapple Press, 1995), 144

dynamited out which basically ruined it. Today where the former springs were is but a small trickle of water.

Lanark Village was sold as a paradise to those who wanted to flee the cold north when they retired. A nine-hole golf course was built beside the highway. As a teenager, I used to go there and try to hit balls onto the highway as the traffic passed by. The village prospered for awhile but then seemed to decline, though it still exists today. One of the things they probably forgot to tell the investors about were the salt water mosquitoes and yellow flies.

One memory that has stuck with me through the years involves traveling through Lanark. It was while going through the area that our beagle, Beauregard, usually started to pass gas, the silent but deadly type. It would slowly filter through the car until we had to either stop and get out for a while or stick his rear end out the window for a few miles, two options that we employed quite frequently.

We sometimes stopped at Putnal's Lanark Station to walk the dog, or to buy soft drinks. The owners operated a car repair shop and had written on the wall their creed;

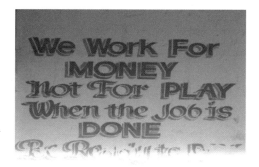

"We work for money not for play, when the job is done be ready to pay"

Quilts

If you drive through Lanark Village today you will see a sign advertising "Hand-made Quilts for Sale by Joy." I stopped there one Valentine's day to see if I could buy one for my wife, as I had forgotten to get anything earlier.

The owner, Joy Guyton showed me around her workshop and unfolded many beautiful quilt designs from which to choose. I found one of some Dutch girls I liked and told her I would take it, but then I got a surprise. Since the quilts were handmade, she said she would have to put me on her waiting list to have my design completed. Thinking it might be a week or so I said OK, only to find out that going on the list meant it would be at least a year before it would be completed. I still ordered it, but my wife had to wait to get that Valentine's gift. I did get her a card that explained everything.

Carrabelle

Four miles from Lanark Village is the city of Carrabelle, or as we called it, "Clara Belle" after a clown on the fifties "Howdy Doody Show."

The town of Carrabelle had its start in 1855 and was incorporated in 1893. Located at the mouth of the Carrabelle River it boasts excellent fishing and hunting. Oliver Kelley moved there in the 1870s and was chiefly responsible for Carrabelle's growth. He named the town after his niece Carrie Hall, who was considered by locals to be the "belle" of the community. In her honor, he named the new town Rio Carrabelle.[81] The town soon became a center for lumber production, naval stores and the rapidly growing seafood industry. Prior to World War I the town prospered but later saw severe economic depression.

---

[81] Morris, *Florida Place Names*, 44

The fishing industry has remained as the primary source of income for area residents. The riverfront grew as a home port for the shrimp fleet and many wholesale and retail seafood houses sprung up on the river banks. Party fishing boats like the "Miss Carrabelle," "Queen of Queens," and the "Barbara Ann" took eager fishermen out to catch a variety of fresh fish in the Florida middle grounds, that area eighty-five miles south of Apalachicola.

During World War II the area saw an influx of soldiers who were sent to Camp Gordon Johnson to be trained for the amphibious assault on D-Day in 1944. The Camp Gordon Johnson Association is remembered today with an annual parade through Carrabelle.

After the war the town went back to being a sleepy fishing town frequented by tourists passing through who stopped at the local Burda's Drug store for a double dipper ice cream cone, to catch the ferry boat named "The Spica" to Dog Island, or to take photos of the World's Smallest Police Station.

A depressed economy resulting from the "Net Ban" of 1995 saw many seafood houses and restaurants close. Only recently has commerce picked up, due largely to the development of the waterfront area with dockage for the deep sea fishing fleet and rental condominiums.

Burda's Rexall

Before there were lots of big drug store chains in Florida there was Rexall Drugs. In a business plan to be copied in future years, they established stores in small communities and became the main place to purchase medicines and sundry supplies. Burda's Rexall was located just off the Coastal Highway and Marine Drive in Carrabelle. It carried beach supplies for sunbathers going to Carrabelle

Beach, or to Dog or St. George Islands. The store also had a lunch counter where customers could enjoy a hamburger or sandwich.

To my family the best thing about it was that they also sold ice cream cones. You could buy a double-decker cone with two scoops side by side and if you could handle it, a double scoop on each side. The ice cream was Meadow Gold whose motto was, "The best is even better". At home, we could only get ice-milk ice cream, so stopping at Burda's for Meadow Gold was a real treat.

The Sting Ray

I remember when I was about 12 years old stopping in Carrabelle at the Gulf gas station on the corner of Marine Drive and Highway 98 (called Tallahassee Road locally). The store was proud to be located near the only traffic light in the city. In actuality it was only a blinking traffic signal that flashed red on Marine and yellow on the highway. The owner told us of a big sting ray that had been caught by a local shrimper and brought to a fish house up the street. Curious, we walked up the block to the fish house to see the sting ray for ourselves.

The fish house was really just a shack made of tin and pitch pine boards which had turned black with age. It hung precariously on the river bank overlooking the dark water. I remember entering to the strong smell of fish and seeing a rough cement floor that glistened with spots of water and fish scales. There were people coming in and out at the back part of the building where the dock was located. It was when looking past the people that I saw the sting ray. It was huge! It lay spread out on the floor, its wing tips touched the walls on each side and its long deadly tail was curled in a circle behind.

The shrimp boat captain was telling everyone the story of his amazing catch. He had been out shrimping the night before and when dropping anchor the next morning he had somehow hooked the sting ray. At first he did not notice anything, but then his boat started moving out to sea. He called to his crew to check his anchor, thinking it must not have set properly and was dragging on the gulf floor. To their surprise, they saw the sting ray swimming ahead of the boat pulling them behind. The captain fired up his engines and tried to back up but the ray still swam on. Frantic, the captain continued to fight the big sting ray, increasing the power of his engines until they whined and strained against the pull of the creature. Finally, the sting ray tired and the shrimp boat started gaining in the game of deep sea tug-of-war. They were able to pull up the anchor with the creature still dangling over the side of the boat. Block and tackles were rigged with a line and the ray was pulled onto the fantail of the shrimp boat.

One of the crew then shot it with a shotgun that the captain kept in his cabin, normally using it to dispatch sharks that occasionally got entangled in the nets with the catch. Not believing what had happened they headed into port to tell the story and show off their catch. I stared at the ray and marveled at the captain's story, knowing that the next time I went out fishing the same would probably happen to me—but the sting ray would be even bigger.

Cop in-a-box

The World's Smallest Police Station was erected in Carrabelle on March 10, 1963. Prior to it being put in place, a police call box had been bolted to a building on Hwy 98. However a problem had developed when local citizens and tourists started using the police phone to make free long distance calls. It was decided to move the call box to another location, but the calls still continued.

When the phone company was replacing an old phone booth at the nearby Rexall drug store, it was noticed that when the policeman answered calls, he had to stand out in the elements. A solution to stopping citizens using the phone, and to make shelter for the policeman was reached by putting the police phone in the old phone booth. Some people still used the phone illegally so later the dial was removed to stop any outgoing calls. The booth got the city a lot of attention around the world for its unique claim. Although it is no longer used as such today, The World's Smallest Police Station still stands, minus the police phone that used to be inside.

Tate's Hell

A local area of some fame is Tate's Hell, a large tract of swampland outside Carrabelle, now owned by the state of Florida. The legend of Cebe Tate, its namesake, was immortalized in the song *Tate's Hell* written and sung by Will McLean.[82]

In 1885 farmer Cebe Tate left from Sumatra and went into the swamp hunting a panther which had killed some of his cattle. Armed only with a shotgun and accompanied by his hunting dogs, he went deep into the swamp and soon became lost. He was bitten by a rattlesnake and in a delirium, wandered for days through the swamp waters filled with snakes, alligators and mosquitoes. He finally stumbled out of the swamp in a clearing near Carrabelle, some 38 miles from where he had started. His hair had turned white from his ordeal. He lived long enough to tell his rescuers his name and that he had just come from "Hell." The name stuck and the 140 acre tract of swampland has since been called Tate's Hell.[83] For the brave, there are now walking trails through the area.

---

[82] Will McLean is called the "Father of Florida Folk. His song *Tate's Hell* was released in January of 1972

[83] Allen Morris, *Florida Place Names*, (Sarasota: Pineapple Press, 1995), 236

Wasting Away in a Wobble Box

When a new officer was hired to work for the Florida Marine Patrol, they normally would not be assigned to where they lived. This was done for two reasons: one to allow the officer to get a start in a new location where the agency could evaluate their effectiveness in a different environment, and second not to put them in an area where they might be enforcing the law on their former friends and acquaintances.

As the state population grew and the economics of causing a new officer to move became greater, this practice was abandoned where possible. We still had duty stations that were hard to fill such as the Florida Keys and Miami, therefore, at times, new personnel were still sent there. Regardless, once an officer had worked in an area for a year he could request a transfer back home or as close as possible, providing a position was available.

If a transfer assignment was close to home but not quite there, the officer would buy or rent a place to live in during the week then go home to his family on days off. One such arrangement was made by Officer John "Bubba" Joyner whose family lived outside of Tallahassee. He rented a travel trailer on St. James Island that he promptly named the "Wobble Box" after the way it wobbled on its foundation when a stiff wind blew. To call the place a home was a stretch. It was only big enough for a small bed, couch, a few chairs and a table. The bathroom was a small cramped room that would have made a better closet.

Sometimes Bubba would take in a friend who was having problems and needed a place to stay. Officer John Erickson was such a friend in need. His wife of one year had left him, which after finding her in bed with another man, was alright with him. He and his soon to be ex-wife had been staying in a trailer her father owned so when they broke up he had to find a place to stay. Bubba had offered him the couch, and having nowhere else to go he had said "Thanks, I'll take it."

Erickson had been staying in the Wobble Box for about a month when one Friday evening he heard a knock on the door. Upon opening the door much to his surprise there stood his estranged wife, Julie.

"Bet ya didn't expect to see me did you?" she asked. "*Hell no*" thought John, but he replied "What do you want, Julie?"

"Well, she said, "I feel badly about how we ended it and just to show you how sorry I am, I baked your favorite chocolate cake." She walked back to her truck and got a container with a huge triple-decker cake and brought it back to him. He took it and mumbled "Thanks", then she got in her truck and drove off.

Bubba, who had been sitting inside, came out and saw the cake container and said," Let's eat some."

Bubba and John went inside and cut huge pieces. It was so good they ate three fourths of the cake in one sitting. John Erickson could not believe the turn of events, here he had been feeling so down and heartsick the past month and now he was eating his favorite cake. What luck.

A summer storm came blowing across the bay and they decided to stay inside, watch a little television and finish the cake. After watching a few shows they turned off the lights and went to bed. Around midnight John started feeling sick. His head swam and his guts ached. He made his way into the small cramped bathroom to relieve himself.

To the uninitiated, you need to understand that one couldn't just walk in and sit down on the toilet like one would normally do. The floor to the bathroom had long since rotted out. All that was left were a couple of two by fours on each side of the wall and two more that held the toilet. You had to brace one foot on the two by four on one wall and the other foot on the one by the opposite wall before sitting down. The roof had a few holes in it that allowed rain to come in but most of it was stopped by a tarp Bubba had placed there during dry weather.

John braced himself, lowered his drawers and sat down. When he did his bowels erupted. Spasms of pain shot through him and he felt like his intestines were burning. Waves of nausea swept over him, and then he heard Bubba knocking on the door telling him to hurry up because he had to go—bad.

Then it struck him, his wife had tricked him. She had baked him a cake laced with Ex-lax, a strong chocolate-colored laxative. She really had showed him how "sorry" she was. He cursed her in his pain and looked to the ceiling where the rain was dripping in. Sitting there he realized he had hit bottom. His heart and his gut ached. He was wasting away physically and mentally over someone who would do such a thing to him. Right then and there he decided it was time to turn his life around. As he was about to shout out to Bubba that they had been duped, the tarp filled with rainwater came crashing down on his head. It was not his day.

It was a week before John and Bubba could even think about going back to work. Both lost about ten pounds and almost came to blows over who got to go in the bathroom and who had to go outside. Later, John swore it had been one of the worst weeks in his entire life. He and Julie went to court for the divorce and she sat there smirking all through the proceedings. If anyone ever asks him about his ex-wife he just replies that he had gotten her out of his system.

I'll Be Watching You

Donald Smith is a friend and colleague of the Florida Marine Patrol and the Fish and Wildlife Commission. One thing you learn about Donald not too long after meeting him is that he has a great sense of humor, and lives to hunt. He has some other qualities I won't mention but those who know him could readily fill them in.

He and his brother grew up in Leon County hunting on all the old plantations. Not that he was invited to do so; it was just that they were a good place to get game. In later years he befriended most of the owners and now is regularly invited to hunt there.

Donald has hunted all over the world and a lot of the big game mounts on display in local gun shops are his. He has a trophy room from his African hunts at his home, but many mounts are still in the countries where he shot them, as he was unable to get them out, due to laws and requests for exorbitant graft payments. He has shot elephants, deer, water buffalos, ostriches and horses but the slickest prey he has every hunted was a crow.

Donald told me the story of his quest to kill a crow one day as we were driving from Perry to Carrabelle on Highway 98. I had just gone by a crow standing on the side of the road when he said "You could have killed that crow if you tried." I said something about how they usually don't stand so close to the roadside and that got him to talking.

"It's always frustrated me how a crow will stand right on the very edge of the blacktop then hop off to the shoulder when you drive up" he said. "I have tried to hit a few but they always hop away or fly before you get to them." I had noticed that but before I could say so, he continued.

"One fall day when I was going home to Mashes Sands, I passed an old crow standing on the other side of the road. It was right after the Alligator Point road in that long stretch before you get to the Ochlocknee River Bridge. I noticed, as I blew by him, that he appeared to be sleeping, as his head was tucked in his wing. I turned around, revved up my engine and headed straight for the crow. I got the car up to about 75 mph. As I was approaching him closer and closer he was still standing there."

"To insure a good hit, I straddled the edge of the road and the pavement, putting the crow square in the middle of the car frame. Faster and faster! Closer and closer! That crow was mine!" He stopped for a minute to remember the rush he had as he approached the hapless crow. Then he became quiet.

"And" I said, "then what happened?"

"Well", he replied, "That wily crow had not been sleeping at all, he was just peering at me from under his wing when I first went by. I am sure he was saying "Here comes that idiot Smith again, guess I'll show him."

Well" I asked?

He gave a sigh then said, "That son-of-a-bitch waited till I was just about on him then did a four foot hop out of the way of my car. I tried to compensate for his movement but went into a spin-out in the grass. That damn thing near about killed me! Then he flew off cawing—laughing I guess."

After I stopped laughing, he added, "I eventually got one, though."

"Really," I replied,

"How?"

"It wasn't that much," he said. "I was coming home one day and a crow was standing in the road and I just hit it, killed it dead. But I figured it must have been sick or something, probably just standing there to commit suicide. "But" he added "I did finally kill one!"

CHAPTER FIVE- FRANKLIN COUNTY

DOG ISLAND TO APALACHICOLA

Dog Island

The original name of Dog Island was Isle auv Chiens, French for Isle of the Dogs.[84] It was so named because the shape resembled a crouching dog. Over seven miles long and covering 2,000 acres, it is the first of four barrier islands on the gulf coast from Carrabelle to Port St. Joe.

A lighthouse was built on the island in 1839 to guide ships through the West Pass which lies between Dog and St. George Islands but it was destroyed by beach erosion. A second lighthouse was built which was destroyed by a hurricane in 1873. Instead of rebuilding another, it was decided to move it to a safer location on the Crooked River in Carrabelle.

During the Civil War the island was used as a staging area for the Union blockade of Apalachicola. In the Second World War it was used by the army to train soldiers from Camp Gordon Johnston.

Located 3.5 miles off shore from Carrabelle, an automobile ferry named *Spica* used to run to the island but was discontinued in 1981.[85] The only way to get to the island today is by boat or private plane. During the hurricane season, when one is threatening the island, the Florida Marine Patrol would dispatch our 82 foot vessel the "J.J. Brown" to evacuate residents who needed to get to

---

[84] Allen Morris, *Florida Place Names*, 70

[85] *Spica* is the name of the brightest star in the Virgo constellation. The ferry that serviced St. George Island was named *Sirius* after the "Dog star" in the Canis Major constellation; it is also the brightest star in the night sky.

the mainland.[86] Today the secluded island is owned by the Nature Conservancy along with local homeowners.

Once a year, on Memorial Day weekend, the tranquility of the island is disrupted by a drunken party that has become known as the "White Trash Bash." The event started as a small affair in 1989 but since 1996 has become a well attended boater and booze party much to the chagrin of the 100 homeowners who live or have places on the island.

Boats loaded with "white trash" revelers from Panama City to Tallahassee come to the island to get drunk, act irresponsibly, and look at pretty girls. The Florida Marine Patrol makes most of their drunken boat operator arrests for the year during this event.

Eastpoint

Eastpoint was established in 1896 by David H. Brown and named for its location on the east point of a peninsula across the Apalachicola River from Apalachicola.[87] A cooperative community was set up by Harry C. Vrooman called the Co-Workers Fraternity at East Point. They profited from their lumber, fishing and manufacturing businesses. It was connected to Apalachicola by the John Gorrie Bridge in 1935.

The locals in Eastpoint are mainly employed in the oyster, crab and fish houses as harvesters, packers or pickers. The first thing that hits you when you arrive in Eastpoint is the pungent smell of fish permeating the air. Piles of oyster shells dry along the banks and oyster boats are docked in the lagoon outside the fish houses.

---

[86] The Florida Marine Patrol vessel is named after Colonel John Joseph Brown former head of the Division of Law Enforcement of the Department of Natural Resources.
[87] Allen Morris, *Florida Place Names*, 74

You can tell a local by his footwear, a pair of white rubber boots called by some "Eastpoint Nikes." Actually, this is an improvement for some as many were known to wear no shoes at all, usually due to of lack of funds rather than desire.

There used to be an intense dislike and rivalry between the residents of Eastpoint, Carrabelle and Apalachicola. This dislike extended to such an extreme in some cases that inbreeding became frequent, with those who would rather marry a cousin than someone from another city, something one could note by the presence of an extra digit on the hand. Of the three cities, Eastpoint seemed to be the most prevalent in this practice. It also made it dangerous to criticize someone as you never knew if he or she was related to the person you were talking with.

Today the area is declining. Oyster packers still ship fresh oysters to markets around the world, but that way of life is disappearing. Generations of families who have spent their lives on the water now see their children leaving the gulf to seek other jobs. This demise is mainly due to seeing their livelihood diminished by increased regulations and changing environmental conditions brought on by development.

Hurricane Dennis hit the area in 2006 with high tides that destroyed some of the old fish houses and many were never rebuilt. Attempts have been made to build a resort on the waterfront but many are against the development, fearing it would threaten the last vestige of the fishing industry located there. Instead of fishing, young people are going into jobs as correction officers or support personnel in the burgeoning prison industry of rural north Florida.

Only in a "R" Month

During oyster season we always stopped in Eastpoint to get a bag of oysters. Any good Floridian knows that you only buy oysters in the "r" months and my dad was one of them. While this later proved to be false, people reasoned that a month with an "r" in it was usually a winter month when oysters were fat and delicious, so the tale didn't hurt — except when summer oyster bars were later opened.

When I was fourteen, I remember my father and I stopping at an oyster house and being greeted by an oysterman and his ten-year old son. The boy eyed us up and down while my dad bought a bag of oysters. Finally he asked me "How old are you?" I told him, and then he thought for a minute and said, "Come back in a couple years and I'll whip your ass!" I tried not to laugh — I was already closing in on six feet tall and outweighed him by about 60 pounds and in two years would be even bigger. But it did say something about people from Eastpoint — they were not afraid of anything.

St. George Island

Author's family at the beach, photo by Bettye Atkinson

St. George Island is a 29 mile long barrier island which is one mile wide at its widest point. It is the largest of the four barrier islands located off the gulf coast between Carrabelle and Apalachicola, Florida. St. George Sound and the Gulf of Mexico border its east end and the West Gap or Bob Sikes Cut on its western end separates it from Little St. George. "The Cut" as it was referred to by locals was built in 1954 to create a ship channel and provide easy access from the bay to the gulf for fishing boats from Apalachicola. Some say the Spanish named the island after St Jorge the Dragon Slayer, one of their saints, others say it was named after the patron saint of England. [88]Before the toll bridge to the island was built in 1965, the only way to get to the island was by ferry boat.

---

[88] Allen Morris, *Florida Place Names,* 211- The Spanish St. Jorge was known as the Dragon Slayer, the Cross of the English St. George is prominent in both the National and Union flags of England.

The Island has been owned by many different individuals, one of them being my step-uncle, Clyde Atkinson. Clyde was an attorney in Tallahassee, Florida in the early 1930s through the 80s. Many times when representing people in legal matters, he would take land as payment for his services. It was not long before he became a major landowner in the Leon County area.

It was through his representation of a famous local citizen of Apalachicola, William Lee Popham, that he came to own the island. Popham had moved to Apalachicola in the early 1900s with the idea of developing an oyster farm to raise and ship oysters to markets around the country. To finance his idea he created a co-op called the Oyster Growers Cooperative Association.[89] Popham started a newspaper called the Oyster Farm News.[90]

He offered shares in his company to investors making promises of great returns. Because he offered these shares through the mail, he got into trouble with the state shellfish commissioner, T.R. Hodges, and the federal government for using the mails to commit alleged fraud.[91] Uncle Clyde defended him in court but eventually lost and Popham was sentenced to two years in jail. Out of money due to the cost of his legal battles and the demise of his oyster farming business, he had to sign over the island property to pay his legal bills.

In the early 1960s Uncle Clyde tried to sell lots at the Island offering them first to friends and family. My parents and grandmother each bought one, though my parents later had to let it go as they could not afford the $25.00 a month payments. Many Tallahassee families bought a lot there hoping to make money off their investments, but the

---

[89] William Warren Rogers, *Outposts on the Gulf*, (Gainesville: University Presses of Florida,1986), 186
[90] Ibid., 200.
[91] Ibid., 220.

Island was slow to develop due to its access being limited to a ferry boat.

After the bridge was built, Uncle Clyde and his partner, Mr. Bill Wilson, sold the island to John Stocks. By the time things finally started developing on the island, most of the original owners had already sold their lots for little or no profit. My grandmother had held onto hers though and it was later deeded to my family.

Clyde had built himself a concrete block house on the east end of the Island in the early 1950s on what is now called East Gorrie Drive. At that time the developed area of the Island consisted of a paved road coming onto the Island from the ferry dock to the main lime-rock road named Gorrie Drive. The paved road divided the island into east and west, the terminus of the roads east end was 11th Street and the west end was 12th Street (where the entrance to the Plantation is today.) At both points there was a beach access road where you can then drive either west to "The Cut" or east to "Sugar Mountain".[92] We spent many days on the Island at Clyde's house when I was growing up and it was here that I first came to love the beaches of the "forgotten coast."

It became a family tradition to spend Easter weekend at St. George Island. We were confident that even though we had to catch the ferry boat before its last run at 5:30 each afternoon, the Easter bunny would somehow deliver our jellybeans and chocolate covered coconut cream eggs. One Easter we forgot to bring our baskets home with us and later found out that both real and candy eggs can sure make a mess when left in a house without air conditioning for a couple weeks.

---

[92] Sugar Mountain was a name we gave to the large sand dunes on the east end of the Island, unfortunately most of the large dunes have disappeared due to hurricanes.

Clyde's house is still there today and looks much the same as I remember, save for the front and back screened porches that are now enclosed. The "servant quarters" bedroom off the back porch is no longer used as such. Clyde had owned two motels (the Skyline and the Southernaire) in Tallahassee and when he came to the beach he'd bring one of the custodians with him to clean and cook. The custodian stayed in his servant quarters. Clyde's daughter, Sara, and her grandchildren now use it as a rental called "*Mimi's Place*" after his wife, Elizabeth Atkinson.

St. George is truly a paradise. The east end of the Island that we named "Sugar Mountain" due to its large sand dunes was later bought by the state of Florida and turned into Dr. Julian G. Bruce St. George Island State Park. The big sand dunes on the island made it a great place to drive "dune buggies", old cars stripped down to tires and a chassis with souped-up engines. We used to hunt on the island in the fall, shooting doves that swarmed by the hundreds in the trees and ducks that frequented the saltwater ponds filled by the ebb and flow of tides.

The St. George Island Ferry

Ferry Boat "Spica" which will soon be put into service.

The "Spica" photo from the State Archives of Florida

The St. George Island ferry started operations in 1955. The first ferry was named "Georgia Boy" but it was later replaced by two state owned ferries the "Sirius" and the "Spica." They had been named after two heavenly bodies, Sirius the Dog Star, brightest star in the sky, and Spica the luminary of Virgo. The "Spica" built in 1949, mainly served Dog Island though it had seen service to St. George as well. The "Sirius" built in 1950, was the main ferry to St. George.

Both ferries were identical. They were bought secondhand from Sunrise Ferries in New York City that had used them to make the eight minute run across the

Hudson River.[93] Sixty-five feet long by forty feet wide, each was powered by two 671 GM diesel engines. The engines were connected to eight Browning "V-belt" drives that turned the propellers.

The ferry required a minimum of five and a half feet of water to operate and had a tunnel running down its center which enclosed the drive shaft. Built with a propeller and rudder on each end, it could be difficult to steer. Designed to hold nine cars, it sometimes held as many as twelve, depending on size. Two crews, each consisting of a captain and an engineer, manned the ferry, working three days on, three days off.

The ferries were initially operated by Franklin County but problems with collecting fares and keeping schedules arose and it was soon turned over to SGI Gulf Beaches Incorporated, a corporation formed by Bill Wilson and Clyde Atkinson, principal owners of the island. Their bookkeeper, George Bradford, was responsible for hiring the ferry crews and daily business operations. A business office was located on the island above the Island Inn store that was run by Fred Hill.

The St. George Island ferry mainland dock was located at Cat Point outside Eastpoint. The ferry route to the island took forty-five minutes and followed a semi-circular course from Cat Point around the oyster bars in the bay, to the St. George ferry dock where the present day bridge now meets the island.

After making a run, the crew waited on the island for forty-five minutes for fares, then loaded up and returned to Cat Point. The process was then repeated on the mainland. In the summertime, six trips a day were made; they were reduced to four after Labor Day until spring. The owners were insistent that the schedules be kept. The

---

[93] Arthur G. Adams, *The Hudson through the Years*, (New York: Fordham University Press, 1996)

122

only exceptions were the last runs on Sundays. No one wanting to leave the island was to be turned away, and the ferry made as many runs as necessary to get them back to the mainland. Florida had not yet gone to daylight savings time when the ferry was running. Therefore many of the last day's trips were made in the dark of night.

The ferry schedule was published in the local papers so beach goers could plan out their trip, making sure to arrive at the dock on time.

FERRY SIRIUS
DAILY SCHEDULE - NOW IN EFFECT
MONDAY THRU THURSDAY

LEAVE MAINLAND	LEAVE ISLAND
7:30 A.M.	9:00 A.M.
10:30 A.M.	12:00 A.M.
1:30 P.M.	2:30 P.M.
4:00 P.M.	5:00 P.M.

FRIDAY - SATURDAY - SUNDAY

7:30 A.M.	8:30 A.M.
9:30 A.M.	10:30 A.M.
11:30 A.M.	12:30 P.M.
2:00 P.M.	3:00 P.M.
4:00 P.M.	5:00 P.M.
6:00 P.M.	7:00 P.M.

St. George Island

A one way ticket cost seventy-five cents for a car and driver with an extra twenty-five cents for each additional passenger. Cars lined up at the dock and when the ferry arrived, the engineer collected the money and then the first nine would be brought on board. The ferry was loaded with cars along each side first, and then the middle aisle would be filled. They loaded it this way so they could accommodate the most cars.

If there were smaller cars in line, the engineer sometimes called one of them to the front and fit them on first. Sometimes people got mad at him for taking cars further back in line not realizing that he was only trying to maximize his load. A smaller car, like a Nash Rambler or Volkswagen, could be put near the sides then "bounced" over into a small space by the railings, making space for another car. The maximum number of cars they could transport at one time was twelve.

The ferry was the island's only link to the outside world for many years. While there was electricity on the island, there were no telephones. The captains of the ferry were often called by Mr. Hill on his portable radio and asked to bring over medical supplies, groceries or other emergency items that might be needed.

It took a special person to captain the vessels. These were true boatmen who knew how to navigate the waters of Apalachee Bay under any conditions. Many thought they could qualify but when they tried to run the vessel with its two propellers and rudders and hold it in a straight line, or come into the dock, they found it would not react as easily as they thought and gave up. Fortunately, the corporation was able to staff the ferries with some of the best boat captains around.

The St. George Island ferry was captained by Carroll McLeod with David Marchant as his engineer. Marion Wing, Buddy Robinson and Joe "Snooky" Barber also piloted the vessel. Milton Kelly and his brother operated the Dog Island ferry. They filled in for each other from time to time to make extra money. All were kind men who faithfully transported many a family to the Islands.

Captain McLeod

Mr. Carroll McLeod was one of the earliest captains of the St. George Island ferry. Before piloting the ferry, he used to run the movie projector at the theater in Apalachicola. He also was very adept at electronics and operated a repair shop there. Realizing that he would soon be out of a job, he left the ferry three months before it ceased operating to take a job with the federal government at the Vitro site on Cape San Blas.

Captain Barber

Joseph Wesley "Snooky" Barber was born in Apalachicola and lived in the area most of his life, leaving only to go into the Navy in World War II, and later to commercial fish in Pensacola. He got the nickname, "Snooky", from his brother to whom he had returned the favor, calling him, "Butch." He explained years ago, that everyone had a nickname.

After ten years of commercial fishing for snapper and grouper which took him away from his growing family, he realized he either "had to get rid of the boat or his wife."

Returning from Pensacola, he and his wife, Erma, raised five children in a home he had bought on Apalachicola Bay. He lived in the same house for forty-four years. It was only recently that he sold it and moved to Carrabelle.

"Snooky" was originally hired as an engineer on the St. George ferry in 1960, working with Captain McLeod. With the retirement of Captain Marion Wing, who ran the second crew, Barber finally got his chance to become a captain. He then hired Joe Hathcock to work as his engineer. I met with Captain Barber at his home in Carrabelle to learn more about him and the St. George Island ferry.

When I sat down to talk to Captain Barber it quickly became obvious that I needed to be prepared to stay awhile.[94] He rattles off stories of days gone by like it was yesterday, each one full of details to delight the imagination. I asked him to tell me about his time running the ferry and sat with him for hours as he reminisced.

He told me that the captains and mates on the ferry always considered themselves "goodwill ambassadors" for the island. They were always willing to talk with their

---

[94] Personal interview with Captain Barber at his home February 2008

passengers and let their kids come up in the pilot house for the ride across the bay.

Island vacationers met the first ferry every morning to buy a newspaper from the rack Snooky had placed aboard so they could stay up with the news. Frequently passengers would give them produce from their gardens or money to thank them for their courtesies. Often it came in handy for Captain Barber to have some extra dollars or food when raising a family of five.

When the ferry was broken and people had already come to the docks expecting to get to the Island, Snooky arranged for a friend in East Point to take them to the island on his personal boat. He told the car owners to give him their keys and he would bring their cars over when the ferry was repaired. True to his word, he and his mate would then load the cars and take them across, parking at the landing for the owners to pick up later.

Summer times were always the busiest. The biggest day Snooky ever had consisted of a total of 86 cars and 375 people. He once transported a house that had been cut in half to be reassembled on the island. The largest load, however, was one of the ferry's last runs when he brought a loaded semi-truck, a dump truck full of gravel, and three cars.

Snooky told me he'd had seen a lot of things and learned a lot about people running the ferry. One of his most embarrassing moments happened when a woman came running down the dock as he pulled away from the island and shouted for him to bring her some Kotex. He was temporarily flustered but soon regained his composure and shouted back, "Do you want regular or king size?"

Once he took a man over to the island who had told him to be sure to save a spot for him on the last ferry as he had to get back to town that night. When it came time for his last run he waited but the man did not show. Concerned, he sent someone to check the house where the man had gone. They found him lying dead from an apparent heart attack beside his car which was stuck in the sand. The information was relayed back to Snooky and he radioed the Sheriff's office. They asked if he could put the man's body in his car and bring it back to the mainland. He agreed to transport the body and the Sheriff's office said they would be at the Cat Point ferry dock to meet him.

When he arrived at the ferry docks there was no deputy to be seen. Snooky had to wait with the body for an hour and a half until they showed up. By that time he was mad and he let them know he did not appreciate having to babysit a dead man. The only other time he brought a body from the Island was when a surf fisherman had been struck and killed by lighting. The Sheriff's office was there to meet him that time.

Teenage girls in bathing suits liked riding with him in the pilot house. One day the ferry was passing by where they were driving pilings for the new bridge, and he asked the girls if they wanted to see how they could stop the pile driver. They asked him "how?" and he told them to stand out on the deck as the ferry passed the pile-driver operator. As promised, when the ferry with the two young beauties went by him, the operator stopped his machine to gawk at the girls.

Snooky worked on the St. George Island ferry until it was retired and replaced by a toll bridge in 1965. The bridge was named after Bryant Patton, a three term legislator from Apalachicola who passed legislation allowing county commissions to build bridges to islands and who also worked to have the Bob Sikes Cut built. The locals called it the "Two Dollar Bridge" after the cost of the toll. The Dog Island ferry Spica ran until April 30, 1982 when it too was retired. Snooky said he made the last run to St. George Island on December 14, 1965. Because the ferry still had to have a licensed captain aboard, he continued manning the vessel for a couple of months after the bridge had opened.

The Sirius was eventually sold to a pulpwood company on the Chattahoochee River that used it to ferry lumber trucks across the river. The last time he saw it was when he piloted it to Panama City to be pulled out of the water for repairs before the sale.

Joseph Wesley "Snooky" Barber is now living with his children in Carrabelle. He likes to ride the woods around the area and to see bears, snakes, otters and deer. Age may have slowed him down a little but he's always willing to spend time talking about the old days.

His life contains the history and stories of the area and he knows that soon they will be lost. In his eyes I could still see a proud young man, the Captain of the Sirius, greeting tourists, asking how they've been since the last time he saw them and telling the kids to stay away from the rails. I was privileged to be able to speak with him and remember my childhood ferry trips to St. George.

Memories of a Kid Riding the St. George Island Ferry

Coming into Eastpoint, we would take a side road to the ferry dock on Cat Point. We'd pull into the parking lot and put our car in line to wait for the ferry to return from the Island. If drivers were in one of the cars that got in line late and could not fit on the ferry's last run to the Island, they'd have to wait until the next day to ride over so we always had to rush to get out of Tallahassee to ensure we'd get there in time. While we waited we'd explore the shoreline, chasing crabs back into their lairs, throwing rocks in the water or visiting with other kids whose family cars were in the line.

The arrival of the ferry was an exciting event. The big boat would blow its horn and the water churned as the engines were maneuvered to dock the vessel. Once the deckhand tied off the vessel, he'd come collect the fares then raise the barrier arm that kept the cars back from the loading ramp. Cars were guided onto the hot steel deck and lined up in threes until the ferry was full. We always looked forward to being in the front three cars as it allowed us to sit in our car and watch out the windshield as we went the four miles across the bay. This also assured that we would be the first off the ferry onto the Island.

On the ferry, the captain let us kids come up into the wheelhouse and see the view as he steered the ferry across the bay. Or we could run around the deck between the cars playing hide and seek or tag. Sometimes we'd climb down the steel rung ladders into the ship's engine room and listen to the steady roar of the diesels pushing the ferry along until we could no longer stand the sounds or the intense heat. I remember standing on the front of the ferry with the wind blowing in my face and thinking about how great it would be to live such a life on the water. Years later I got that chance when I became a Florida Marine Patrol officer.

"Sarge"

The Cassel's were a retired military family who lived on the Island when I was a kid. Both he and his wife had seen service to our country and had traveled all over the world before settling down on the Island. Her name was Delores and everyone just called him "Sarge".

Sarge was the local jack of all trades who could fix a pump, get a hot water heater working or pull a car out of the sand. He also had three dune buggies he'd rent to visitors.

Every day Sarge met the ferry boat captains on their layovers and took them back to his house for coffee and conversation. When he left his house, whether to go to the ferry docks or some other errand, his mongrel dog followed behind his jeep. Sarge never picked him up, but the dog still ran after him. I guess he had figured out that wherever Sarge was going, since they were on an island, it could not be too far.

The dog was part German Shepherd and Labrador. Sarge called him Mike. His hair was dirty and matted and stood in spikes. He had been born with a deformity of his mouth that made him look like he was snarling at you. He'd sit by Sarge's jeep and wait till he was done with whatever errand he was on. Then he'd run home behind him. Even though Sarge was one of the nicest people you ever met, most people steered clear of his Jeep when that dog was around.

Turtle Crawl

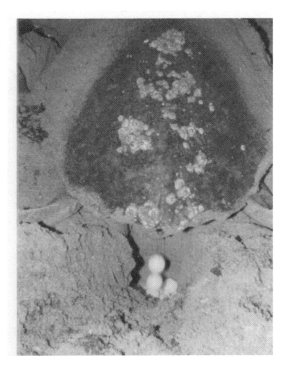

Loggerhead turtle laying eggs on beach, photo by author

My father rented a dune buggy from Sarge Cassel when we went to the Island to fish at the Cut or joy-ride on the beach. Years later we bought our own Jeep and we'd spend days and nights driving over the dunes, up and down the beaches, feeling the exhilaration of salty wind and an occasional spray in our faces as we drove.

It was one of Sarge's dune buggies that took me to see my first turtle-crawl, the annual pilgrimage of Loggerhead, Kemps Ridley, Green and Leatherback turtles that crawled up the beach to lay their eggs. My father had told us about the turtles, how they'd slowly come onto shore, crawling to the highest point on the beach where they could safely lay their eggs. He told us about the large tears they'd cry, a mother's lament for the babies she'd never see, and how, when finished, she'd lovingly cover the nest and try to camouflage it from predators that were sure to come.

Late one July night when I was about seven years old, my father woke me and my sisters, telling us he had found a turtle on the beach. He had been out driving on the beach looking for telltale tracks that looked like the tire of a tractor in the sand. We quickly dressed and loaded into the dune buggy. As we drove down the moonlit beach we could hear the waves crashing on the beach and see the ghost crabs skittering away from the headlights of the buggy. Soon we arrived at the turtle track, one set of large deep ruts cut into the sand by the turtle's flippers that led up to where the turtle was digging her nest.

My father had told us that once she was on her nest and had begun laying, she'd not leave until done, but if we disturbed her before she started, she'd go back out to sea and try again later in another location.

We quietly walked up the beach and there before my eyes was a large conical shaped shell of a 300 pound loggerhead turtle, mossy green with a few large ragged barnacles attached. The turtle's massive head was pointed towards the sea and her flippers would rise up with each strain as she pushed out her eggs. My father went around behind her and dug into the area where she was laying her eggs into a smooth, deep hole dug by her flipper. The hole was slowly filling up with white ping pong ball shaped eggs which were emerging from the turtle three and four at a time mixed with a yellow gold slime. He plucked one out of the nest and let us feel its leathery texture, then held it up to his flashlight to show the yolk inside before carefully replacing it in the nest.

I looked at the turtle's eyes and saw the tear tracks down her face just as my father had said there would be. It was one of the most amazing things I had ever seen. We stood back and watched the turtle finish laying her eggs and then saw her slowly start to cover them with her back flippers, moving piles of sand to fill the hole then patting it, moving in a circular motion over the nest. The flippers were throwing sand in all directions to disguise the location of the nest. I tried to keep my eyes focused on the exact spot where the eggs had been laid but was soon unable to tell exactly where it was.

Her job done, the turtle laboriously crawled back towards the sea, each dig of the flipper moving her closer to the water and an opportunity to rest after her busy night. My father stood on her back as she moved towards the water, looking like Poseidon as he rode sea creatures in the water, but we begged him to get off, feeling she had been through enough that night. I watched as the turtle slowly disappeared into the foaming waters, her tracks being washed away by the surf. Right then, I knew that I had been given a glimpse into the wonder of Florida's natural resources and feeling that I would want to be a part of protecting them.

As a Florida Marine Patrol officer, I had many chances to protect these gentle sea creatures. Walking the beaches of Ft. Lauderdale in the late seventies, I saw many turtles crawl and helped move the nests out of harm's way. One night I responded to a call of a loggerhead turtle swimming in a condominium's pool. Another time I went to a parking garage swarming with baby turtles that had just hatched. They thought the bright lights of the condo was the moon and had gone the wrong way away from the sea.

Poachers were prevalent then, people who either wanted to butcher the turtle or steal her eggs. The eggs were thought to be aphrodisiacs and sold for a dollar each on the local black market. The eggs were also desired by bakers as the yolks were said to produce light, fluffy cakes.

Crow Calling

When things got slow on the Island and we were looking for something to do, we could always shoot crows at the trash dump. The dump used to be off a back road on the west side of the Island right after the ferry dock. It has since been covered and million dollar homes are built atop the fill, a fact that's probably unknown to their owners.

We had a portable 45 record player and a record that imitated crow calls. One record that always summoned the crows well was titled "Call to Meeting". It was the loudest racket you ever heard, full of crows shrieking and cawing. We placed the record player at the bottom of a trash pile and then we'd hide a safe distance away and wait for the crows to come.

A crow is a very wily bird and is not easily fooled (just ask Donald Smith). To call them up and get a chance to shoot one was good sport. We used a 22 rifle which made it even harder as our shot had to be true. Usually we got one or two before they would figure out what was going on or spot us and fly away. But we always had a good time.

Hi-Ho Silver!

One day when fishing out in front of our beach house, I hooked a tarpon that probably weighed 85 to 100 pounds. The big fish pulled the line so hard it made my teeth vibrate. It jumped up out of the water and tail-walked throwing bursts of silvery blue water in the air before finally breaking the line. I had a couple of the same type lures in my tackle box and quickly tied another on my line casting it out where she had been, hooking her again, then feeling the same sensations as she went through her gyrations to shake the hook. The scenario was repeated once more until I was out of lures and she was no longer interested playing with me. She returned to the depths of the Gulf and I soared like a kite at the thrill of my "almost" catch.

Kid's Best Friend

There was a general store on the island called the Island Inn. It never really had much merchandise, just a gas pump, sundry items, cigarettes, drinks and candy. We used to walk up the beach to the store, buy candy and play the pinball machine on the porch.

The store was really just a small portion of the SGI Properties' office building. The store had a Dutch door through which the proprietor sold goods and also dispensed local gossip. A screened-in porch running the length of the building, served as the meeting place for visitors and locals. A big poster bulletin board was hung next to the pinball machine, bearing the ferry schedule, tide chart, and pictures of proud fishermen and pretty women displaying their catches.

The owner had a large yellow Labrador retriever that we called St. George. He loved to run on the beach chasing sea gulls, barking with frustration when they flew out of his reach. He also befriended every kid who came near the store. No matter how far we wanted to walk down the beach or how deep we wanted to swim, St. George would go with us. He especially liked it if we had a float, then he would position himself either beside us or completely on it, forcing us to get in the water and pull him along. When he tired of playing, he'd go back to the store and sit on the porch waiting for the next adventure.

Crab Smashing

As kids, one of our favorite beach night pastimes was to go ghost crab smashing. Looking back it probably was not the best ecological thing to do. My step-brother Ricky Atkinson would drive the dune buggy slowly down the beach with us hanging on to the sides looking for the white ghost crabs that had skittered too far away from their holes. When we spotted one, the nearest kid would run and chase it trying to smash it with a stick. Those crabs were fast! We ended up trying to corner them before they hit their hideaways, sometimes chasing one back and forth along the beach until it either escaped or died.

Ghosts on the Coast

When we were at the beach, we'd always build a bonfire one of the nights to cook hotdogs and marshmallows. During the day when we took a break from swimming, we'd walk the beach and haul back driftwood and tree limbs which had washed on shore or in the nearby woods. The wood was piled in a fire pit in a tepee shape and would grow quite some size by nightfall. As the sun started to set we'd set up chairs in a semi-circle around the fire pit. After watching the last rays of sunset spread across the sky in pinks, yellows and blues we'd light the fire.

Helped along by a few pine lighter knots, placed in the midst of the driftwood, the fire sprang to life in the dark night. The wooden tepee glowed like a golden cone as the flames climbed higher and higher on its frame. The adults relaxed in their chairs with a drink, engaging in small talk, while the kids ran around the fire then out to the ring of darkness where the firelight did not penetrate. When the fire burned down to a smaller pile of coals we'd keep it going by adding an occasional log or branch, then we'd cook our dinner.

Each kid would receive a coat hanger they'd have to disassemble and stretch out into a long metal wand. After the initial clash with other kids in a mock sword fight, the hotdogs would be slid onto the end of the now elongated hanger. The hanger would droop like you were leading a puppy on a leash with the hotdog end almost touching the ground. Kids would gather around the fire to roast their hotdogs. Sometimes one would be lost in the fire and would lie there and sizzle, tantalizing the hungry crowd of cooks. When done the hotdogs were placed on waiting buns that our parents had set out on a table with various condiments. Plates would be piled high with baked beans and potato chips. Dixie cups of Kool-Aid were the drink of choice, then everyone would either claim an empty chair or sit cross-legged on the sand around the fire to eat.

After the meal was finished the coat hangers were put back in service to roast marshmallows to make S'mores. S'mores were marshmallows, chocolate squares from a Hershey's candy bar and graham crackers made into a sandwich. They were called such because when you ate one you always wanted some more. I liked my marshmallows golden brown and could never understand why one kid would always set his on fire and watch it burn to a black crisp before eating.

Soon our stomachs would be full and we'd settle around the fire and watch it glow in the night. The cool night-time sea breezes blew just enough to make you want to stay close enough to the pit to feel the fire warmth. If we got too hot we'd move to a more comfortable distance and still enjoy watching the flames flicker. It was then that we'd start telling ghost stories.

There are many different legends and stories concerning Indians, pirates, spirits and fairies that have been told about the Forgotten Coast.

One story was told of the Indian Warrior at Wakulla Springs. Ancient Seminole lore spoke of fairies coming in the still of the night singing and dancing around the edges of the springs. At midnight when the moon was full, they disappeared as a gigantic Indian warrior in a stone canoe rose out of the springs. He carried a large copper paddle. A cloud surrounded him on the waters as he sat there immovable and alone surveying the springs.[95]

Another spoke of Pirates who really had used the waters of the Forgotten Coast to launch raids on merchant ships or to hide from custom's vessels. Their treasure was said to be buried in Money Bayou between Indian Pass and Cape San Blas as well as other sites on the coast. The Pirates assaulted merchant vessels killing all the crew and passengers before looting and burning the ships. I spent many a scary night around the campfire listing to tales of bloody pirates who would sneak up the beach behind you and cut your throat or cart you away to serve as a slave on their ghost ships.

There were tales of ghosts who were said to be seen by frightened passengers trying to hail passing cars or as old maids who walked the hallways haunting their former hotels.[96] All became the main characters in stories designed to frighten us. But none ever topped Eyeballs.

---

[95] Federal Writers Project, *A Guide to the Southernmost State: Florida,*(New York: Oxford University Press, 1944) 130
[96] Must See, Must See Media LLC, Port St Joe, Fl. "Myths and Legends of the Forgotten Coast" 3, no. 1(Spring 2009)

Eyeballs

On different trips to the coast we'd hear stories my father told of these spirits that lived as close as the beach outside our bedrooms, but the one story that scared us most was about "Eyeballs".

Eyeballs stood ten feet tall and his face was covered in blood. He roamed the beaches at night seeking his favorite food — eyeballs. His hands had long bony fingers, each bearing a sharp pointed fingernail. He used his fingernails to scratch on screens and windows of your house until he could get in. Then he would creep into your bedroom and while you were sleeping he'd pluck out your eyeballs and eat them. His victims were cursed to walk the earth blindly searching for their eyes. My father usually saved the story about Eyeballs until last, telling it to us just before we had to go in and get ready for bed.

We'd try to linger around our parents hoping they would not make us go to bed but soon we were tucked in and lights were turned off. Every sound would make us jump; a tree branch scratching on a window would make my sister scream. We lay rigid on our beds afraid to close our eyes just knowing if we did we'd never see again. The night would drag on and when our parents checked in on us before they went to bed they'd find us still wide awake. My mother finally made my father stop telling us that story, but it was only after we had a chance to visit Eyeballs one night in a Tallahassee graveyard.

I remember the night well. It was 1961 and we were enjoying one of those the lazy summer days that every kid longs for during the school year. As we had done since the end of school, we'd get up in the morning around 10:00 and watch "I Love Lucy", "The Real McCoy's", and "The Andy Griffith Show" while we ate sugar cereal. After the shows were over we'd get dressed and go outside to play, staying out until our parents came home at 5:30. We'd get a quick bite of dinner then go out to play until dark, catching fireflies until it was so dark we couldn't see. We'd play kick the can, hide and seek and "freeze tag" with the car lights coming down the road.

This particular July night my sisters were attending a neighborhood slumber party at the Odom's house across the street. My best friend Mike Cook was staying with me. A co-worker of my mom's and her husband were over for a cook-out. My dad called them Skeeter and Nita, he was a law student and she worked as a clerk with Mom.

The adults were sitting on the front porch and Mike and I were playing in the yard when the girl's from the slumber party came over to see my Dad. They had been telling scary stories and my sisters had told them about Eyeballs. My dad told them that he could take them to see Eyeballs if they wanted to meet him. The girls looked around at each other nervously, and as often happen in groups someone said "OK" and everyone else nodded in agreement. My dad called Mr. Odom telling him he was going to take the kids so he would know where they were, and then everyone loaded into our Rambler station wagon which had two seats facing forward and one facing to the rear. The girls piled into the front seat beside my dad and in the middle seat, while Mike and I sat in the back facing seat. We drove away from the house full of anticipation and bravado, not knowing what to expect.

As we pulled into the Oakland Cemetery on Fourth Avenue and Brunough Streets some of the younger girls decided they did not really want to follow through on this little adventure saying they wanted to go home. "Oh no," said my sister, Terrie, the eldest of the group at 14, "We have come this far we might as well go on." Famous last words if I ever heard them!

We drove through the silent graveyard until we came to the top of a hill. My dad stopped the car and to our left we could see a huge marble mausoleum bearing the name

Hodges. My dad said, "Here we are, who wants to go up to the grave to see Eyeballs with me?" No one volunteered. "Well," said my dad, "We can't leave here unless someone goes up to see him or he will get us all." By now the girls were not too sure this had been such a good idea. My sister, Toni, said she would go with him and we watched them get out of the car and start walking towards the grave. We knew it would be the last time we ever saw either of them alive.

Suddenly a *Whooooo! Whoooo!* came from the grave and everyone in the car started screaming. Toni ran back to the car and quickly got inside while the girls begged my father not to go any further. A couple of girls started to cry and my dad figured he had scared everyone enough for the night. He got back into the car as the sounds from the grave started getting louder and louder. My youngest sister, about 11 at the time, shouted "Let's get the hell out of here!" My dad was so distracted by all the screaming and the sounds coming from the grave that he never said anything about her swearing.

He turned the key to start the engine and nothing happened. He turned it again...nothing. The inside of the car was now pure panic and it got even worse when my father told us he would have to go ask Eyeballs to let us go. Evidently he had killed our battery to keep us from leaving his clutches. Tearful young girls watched as he went across the graveyard to the mausoleum, and then he disappeared behind it. "We all are going to die," screamed the girl who had originally thought it would be a good idea to come to the graveyard. Everyone looked at her and I am sure thought the same thing I did, "If all of us are going to die, you can bet you will be first."

Our faces pressed against the rolled up car windows, we watched and waited for my dad to reappear. Finally we saw him coming towards the car. "Don't let him in," shouted someone. "He's an Eyeballs now too!" My dad came up to the car and shook the door handle telling the girls in the front seat to open the door. Timidly, Toni reached over and pulled up the door lock and he opened the door. Everyone drew back to the other side of the car when he sat down, not knowing what to expect. "It's OK." said my dad, "Eyeballs has agreed to let us go." We all breathed a sigh of relief. "But," he said, "Someone is going to have to push the car down the hill because he will not let the car start in the graveyard."

Because Mike and I were sitting in the back, the girls agreed that we should be the ones to do it. I guess none of them cared if Eyeballs got us anyway. Mike and I decided that we would roll down the rear window just enough for us to slip out and back again, figuring Eyeballs was too big to get in such a small opening. We rolled the window down about 10 inches and climbed out of the car. As soon as we started pushing the car the sounds started coming from the grave again. Mike and I pushed until we were running behind the car as it started down the hill, then we quickly got back in the car. The interior of the car was quiet except for the sound of a few girls sniffling as my dad steered it down the hill and out the gates of the cemetery.

Thinking we were now safe, we told my dad to start the car and take us home, but it still would not start. We did not know what to do. Then as if by magic, my mom and her friend came driving up in my dad's other car. They said they were worried about us since we had not come home. We were more than a little glad to see them. Everyone wanted to just leave my dad and ride home with my mom but that was impossible. The car she was driving was a little Nash compact that only held two comfortably. She told my dad she would go get some jumper cables to help start the car and then left. In about ten minutes she was back and we got the car started and headed for home.

When we got back home, the girls decided they had had enough of the slumber party and chose to go home to their parents. Mike also went back to his house. Everyone had a fitful night's sleep and I'm sure every parent in the neighborhood was upset at my dad for scaring their kids half to death. That was the last time we ever talked about Eyeballs in my house.

The Catcher's Earwigs

When I had children of my own, I never told them the ghost story about Eyeballs, figuring one emotionally scarred generation was enough, but I did tell them a story about earwigs and that scarred them anyway.

As most parents do, they try to recreate some fond memories from their childhood and share them with their children. My wife and I both enjoyed the beach and would take our kids there whenever we could. We rented a house at St. George Island during spring break and built bonfires at night on the beach. My kids would ask me to tell them a story and usually I would try to make up something that included three characters that each one could identify with while not calling them by name. One night they asked me to tell them a scary story.

Before this story none of my children were afraid of things that crept or crawled so I didn't think a story about a little bug would scare them too much. They gathered close around the fire and I began.

"Once there was a man called the "Catcher" who liked to catch things. He'd go out at night roaming all over North Florida looking for something to add to his collection. He carried a big burlap sack and wore an overcoat with deep pockets.

The Catcher caught animals, snakes, bugs and any young children who stayed out playing too late at night. He'd take them to his laboratory where he would perform bizarre experiments on them. He'd take the legs off roaches and put them on rabbits; he cut off children's lips and tongues and replaced them with bird beaks. Opossum tails were transplanted onto birds and children's fingers were sawed off and fed to baby alligators.

Everything he caught he would place in jars or cages so he could watch them. All his captives were fed fish guts and if they would not eat it they were killed and used for food the next day. If any of his "prizes" as he called them, ever escaped he would chase them down and return them to his laboratory. If a child escaped he would go to his or her house. Late at night, creeping into their room he'd release an earwig, something that would torment them for the rest of their lives.

One night a child who had been staying at the beach was caught while sitting around a campfire but had later escaped. When he went to bed that night the Catcher was hiding in his room. After everyone had fallen asleep, the Catcher slid out from under the bed and put a pregnant earwig on the child's pillow. The little red-brown insect with long sharp pinchers then crawled into his ear and burrowed into his brain. A stinky yellow slime dripped out of the child's ear as the bug moved deeper and deeper into his head driving him crazy.

It did not matter if the child's parents took him to the doctor. Because even if the doctor was able to remove the earwig, the pregnant bug laid her eggs all through the child's brain. The child would have to live the rest of his life in the crazy kids ward at Chattahoochee, Fl.

My children listened to my story in absolute silence. I never realized how scared they were until bedtime that night. A small silverfish ran from under one of their pillows and they all started screaming. My wife came in and asked what was going on and I sheepishly told her about the story I had told around the campfire. She looked at me as if I was the dumbest being on earth for telling young children such a tale. I had managed to scare them of bugs, being alone in their bedrooms, things under the bed and having to live the rest of their lives in an insane asylum-all in one story.

We spent the rest of the night in their bedroom trying to get them to calm down and sleep, all the while telling them it was a make believe story. I don't think any of them bought it but they did finally go to sleep. When they woke up in the morning without having gone crazy in the night, everything was alright. Even though my children are now grown and have kids of their own, they still remember the earwig story. I guess it was a good thing I never told them about Eyeballs.

Baby Love

When my children were little there was a television commercial that poked fun at cell phone signal skip. A man would dial his cell phone and another man on the other end, dressed in beach wear, would pick up his phone and say "Fujiyama Beachside". We liked the commercial, and the kids, when asked where they wanted to go on the weekend, would say "Fujiyama Beachside!" which to them meant St. George Island.

We often went to the state park located on the eastern end of St. George island and would walk to the end where we could see the East Pass which separated the island from Dog Island and connected the St. George Sound and the Gulf of Mexico.

One weekend we saw a young doe deer on the beach. My children were amazed when she came right up to us at a distance of only about 10 feet. As we walked the beach, the deer walked with us. One of the kids started calling the deer "Baby" and we all picked up on it and sang the

Supremes' hit *"Baby Love"* to her as we walked down the beach.[97] When we neared the park entrance she decided to go on her way. We waved good-bye to her but the memory lingers. It is one my children still cherish.

After "Baby" left we decided to take a shortcut across the island. It turned out to be a bad move. We were all barefoot and the sand was burning hot regardless of where we stepped. Looking for a cooler route, we decide to go through a slightly vegetated area—bad move again- as the area was filled with sand-spurs. Stuck between the two choices and having three tired, hurting children, I opted for the sand spurs and being barefoot, I carried each one out of the sand spur area separately. That day sticks with my children today, not only because of the "Baby" experience but because they realized a fathers unconditional love first-hand. While my actions that day stuck with my kids, the pricks from those sand spurs stuck with me for quite a while.

He-Coon

We spent many days fishing the pristine gulf waters off St George, either surf fishing in front of the beach house or driving in the dune-buggy westward to the Bob Sikes Cut which was named after a powerful Congressman from Pensacola, Robert F. "He-Coon" Sikes.

If one were to start checking he would find that just about everything built in northwest Florida between 1940 to the 1980s that had any connection to federal funding also had Bob Sikes name on it. The "He-Coon" moniker came from the country lore that denotes the leader that no one messes with because he was "the baddest thing around," and with all his power, Sikes surely was.

---

[97] *"Baby Love"* was recorded by the Supremes in 1964 on the Motown label.

Cape St. George Lighthouse and Keepers cottage,
Authors collection

The Cape St. George Lighthouse

There have been three lighthouses built on St. George but its most durable was the one built in 1853 on a mile wide spit, the widest point on St. George. Manned by lighthouse keepers for 100 years, the light was automated in 1949 ending the need for a keeper.

When Bob Sikes Cut was built in 1954, the portion of the island containing the lighthouse was separated from the main island. It was then that the area started being called Cape St. George or Little St. George. Fishermen fished off the rocks that lined the channel, staying mostly on the main part of the island. Boaters came over to Little St. George to picnic and sunbath in seclusion.

The lighthouse continued in operation until 1994 when it was endangered by erosion from hurricane Andrew. The Coast Guard decided to deactivate the light and the next year tidal surge from Hurricane Opal caused the lighthouse to begin to lean.

For ten years it stood like a drunken sailor on the beach, half standing half falling. It became an icon for the island until it fell into the gulf in October of 2005. A grass roots movement was started to save the lighthouse. Funds were raised to finance moving and reconstructing the lighthouse on the main island where it could be used to promote tourism and the Island's history. Opened in December, 2008, the new smaller version welcomes visitors as they come off the bridge. Little St. George was bought by the Nature Conservancy and made into a state reserve.

Captain Joe "Snooky" Barber's family had at one time owned St. George Island and his grandfather, Edward G. Porter, had been the keeper of the St. George Island Lighthouse from 1893 to 1912. Though his grandfather was no longer the lighthouse keeper when Snooky was born, he remembered, as a child, visiting the lighthouse and spending summers playing on the beach there.

To assist Lighthouse-keeper Porter in carrying food, kerosene and equipment to the lighthouse the government had bought him a red-brown sway backed mare named, Neb, to pull the lighthouse supply wagon. Mr. Porter would hitch up the horse then go down to the quarter mile long government dock to pick up supplies and visitors and take them back to his home beside the lighthouse. A boathouse was located by the dock where he kept his boat. When he returned from trips to the mainland he'd attach a winch cable to each end of the boat and hand crank it out of the water for safe keeping.

The lighthouse-keeper's house was a large four bedroom structure with a fireplace in each room. One of the distinctive things one notices in pictures of the place are the four chimneys. A horse barn for Neb was beside the house as well as a shed where 55 gallon drums of kerosene to fuel the light were kept.

Each day Porter would climb the stairs of the 72 foot lighthouse carrying cans of kerosene to keep the light burning throughout the night. The light at that time was built like a lantern with a mantel that burnt the kerosene. Each day he would have to clean the black smut caused by the burning wick off of the lens. He then would unfurl a thick canvas blanket to place around the glass of the lighthouse, put there to shield the sun's rays from igniting the kerosene.

Though it sounded a little long for a horse to live, Captain Barber said that Neb lived for 48 years, serving as the only transportation on the island until the first military Jeeps were brought over in the forties by Camp Gordon Johnson personnel. The family collected a government paycheck to care for Neb his entire life, making him one of the government's oldest animal pensioners. When he died, Neb was buried near the lighthouse.

"You know those lighthouses were strictly for coastline navigation," said Captain Barber. "When we got off shore all we had was a compass. I spent many years navigating seventy to a hundred miles off the coast of Florida with just my compass. When we came back in we'd just take a compass heading and come on in. When you got closer in you could look for the "gloom" as I called it, that glow from the city lights of Pensacola, Destin or Panama City that you can see from off-shore as you approach. After years of fishing in the coastal waters you learn the bottom and can tell where you are by the water depths etc. But for many years all we had were those compasses. Today they use radar and depth finders and GPSs. We never had anything like that."

The Rooster

There used to be a seafood dealer in Eastpoint that for
years was notorious for cutting corners when it came to
the law. He did whatever he could to get around the
resource laws and because of this he was constantly in
trouble with the Florida Marine Patrol (FMP).

One afternoon our dispatchers received a call that there
were untagged bags of oysters in the dealer's cooler.
Florida law requires that all bags taken out of the bay be
tagged with the harvester's permit number, date and place
harvested. An officer was sent to check out the tip but
when he arrived, the dealer refused to let him see the bags
and placed a padlock on his cooler.

Calling for back-up, the officer waited until a supervisor
arrived to assist. The dealer meanwhile called his friends
to help him stop the officers from coming on his property.
What had started as a routine check was quickly becoming
a lot more. To make matters worse, many of his friends
stopped on the way there and bought beer to shore up
their courage (something commonly called "loud-mouth
soup" based upon its affect on the individual). Back-ups
arrived to help the officer and the dealer was convinced he
needed to open the cooler. Inside were 140 bags of
untagged oysters. The dealer was advised that he was
going to be issued a citation and the oysters seized and
destroyed.

Infuriated, he called to his friends, now half drunk, to
help him. The angry crowd of friends shouted insults at
the officers and threatened them but did nothing else. The
officers began loading the oysters into a dump truck that
had been commandeered from a local agency office,
intending to take them to a place where they could be
destroyed.

When an attempt to move the truck was made, one of
the friends who was called "Rooster" (because of a big

black cowboy hat with a rooster feather he always wore) got down on the ground near the tires and started screaming that the truck had rolled over his leg. The crowd pushed in at the ring of officers that had formed around Rooster to care for him and for a moment it looked like any order was going to be lost. However it was quickly determined that he was not injured at all but was only trying to excite the crowd.

Not wanting to take any chances, an ambulance was called and Rooster was carted away. The dump truck drove away without any further incident to a place where the oysters could be destroyed after the judge signed a destruction order. Rooster was transported to the hospital then released after running up a costly and unnecessary personal bill. While the people of Eastpoint were not afraid of anything — I didn't say everyone was smart.

Boat Diving

Not long after our run-in with the Rooster in Eastpoint, another oysterman was being checked by two FMP officers when he accidently fell off his boat into the water. One of the officers snickered at his fall, trying not to laugh and the man got embarrassed, then mad, and decided to sue the agency.

He filed a lawsuit claiming that the officer's boat had bumped his boat and made him fall overboard. Instead of spending time fighting the charges, the department settled with the fisherman for a minor sum, thereby saving the state time and money. Afterwards, every time a patrol boat came near one of their boats, oystermen were falling overboard, all trying to cash in –I didn't say everyone was stupid either!

Apalachicola

The name Apalachicola was derived from the Hitchite Indian word meaning "the people on the other side".[98] The Choctaw word Apalachi means "allies."

Apalachicola was founded in 1820 and has had many different names. It was originally called Bay Town by the Creek Indians. In the mid 1820s it was called Cotton Town or Cottonton.[99] The town was founded and incorporated as West Point in 1831 due to its geographic location on the Apalachicola River (East Point is on the other side). The city name was formally changed to Apalachicola by the Florida Legislative Council later in 1831.[100]

The city is located in Franklin County which was named after American icon Benjamin Franklin. The county was created out of Washington County in 1832.

Dr. John Gorrie

Most people associated with north Florida know who Dr. John Gorrie was, for those who do not; he was the inventor of the ice machine. Even more importantly his process was derived from trying to find a way to cool rooms for patients with yellow fever. That process is what we today call air conditioning.

Dr. Gorrie practiced medicine in Apalachicola, Fl. He is one of its most famous citizens and more than any other person can be credited with the reason Florida was tamed.

Prior to his invention, the state was known as a wild, bug-infested, sweltering place. When people could come,

---

[98] Allen Morris, *Florida Place Names*, 9
[99] Kevin M. McCarthy, *Apalachicola Bay,*(Sarasota: Pineapple Press, 2004), 60
[100] Harry P. Owens. "Apalachicola: The Beginning", *Florida Historical Quarterly* 47, (July 68-April 69), 282

enjoy the beaches, and then retreat to an air conditioned room, the whole face of tourism and settlement in Florida changed.

Dr. Gorrie should also be noted as a savior for the fishing industry. Prior to his invention of the ice machine, ice was brought by steamer from the north then covered with sawdust to keep it intact. Fishermen were limited in their markets to local areas where the fish could be sold before they spoiled. When ice became readily available they were able to ship their products throughout the state and nation, all due to Gorrie's invention.

I Can't Hear You!

The shrimper stood on the fantail of his boat and pointed at the Marine Patrol officers, he then placed his fingers to his lips, bent over and patted his ass. Even though he was deaf, Martin A. Williams knew how to convey his message.

So opened the latest round of the age old battle between commercial fishermen and what they considered unfair state regulations and those who enforced them. For years there had been controversy surrounding the shrimp count in Apalachee Bay.[101] In the fall when the white shrimp "run", shrimp boats converge on the area. The Florida Marine Patrol would be out in force to take a "shrimp count" before the bay could be opened for fishing.

Officers boarded the boats, weighed and counted five random samples of the catch to see if they met a legal

---

[101] Shrimp count refers to the process of counting the number of shrimp with heads on it takes to make a pound. For enforcement purposes officers would weigh out five random one pound samples of the catch then count the number of shrimp in each pound to determine average size. Florida law designated an allowable count.

count. Shrimp are graded and sold according to size, determined by how many it takes to make a pound. The higher the number it took to make a pound, the smaller the shrimp. In the winter it was not unusual to find the count running too high. If the shrimp were too small, that area of the bay was closed until the count dropped. Because the shrimpers knew they had to fish to pay their bills, they became aggravated whenever the count was determined too high. In defiance, they would continue to shrimp in the area, taking their chances on getting caught versus making a killing at the market. Martin A. Williams was one of those independent minded fishermen who had only two days before been quoted in the local paper saying he was going to "fish the bay no matter what the count or the presence of the Marine Patrol."

The Marine Patrol would call in officers from around the state to assist local officers during the shrimp run season. They stayed at local motels in Apalachicola and worked twelve hour shifts patrolling the bay. A cat and mouse game ensued between shrimpers and the officers. Using radar, shrimpers would trawl along the boundaries of the closed area then make a run into the closed area when they thought no one was watching. Officers aided by aircraft patrolled the areas and ran to a boat when it came into the closed area.

As the officers pulled alongside Williams' boat, he went forward to the wheelhouse and put the boat in gear. One of the officers carrying a set of portable scales quickly jumped aboard as the shrimp boat outriggers started ripping off the canvas top of the officers' patrol boat.

Maneuvering out of the way to avoid further damage to his boat, Officer Ken Clark watched his partner, Officer Herman Jenkins, go up to the wheelhouse and after placing his hands on both sides of the door opening, lean in to talk to Martin Williams. The next thing he saw was Jenkins get hit flush in the face by Williams then the two of them falling to the deck in a scuffle. Officer Clark yelled "10-24, 10-24, officer needs assistance!" and in an instant other officers patrolling the area converged on the shrimp boat.

On board, Jenkins rolled around in the tiny wheelhouse fighting with the burly shrimper. He struggled to gain the upper hand with the shrimper, all the while trying to keep his weapon protected and away from him. Williams grabbed and hit at the officer while his son, who had taken over the wheel of the shrimper, kicked the officer in the back. Soon another officer boarded to assist Jenkins and together they were able to subdue him.

Williams was soon handcuffed. A life jacket was placed on him in case he jumped overboard and he was put in the patrol boat to be transported to the Franklin County jail. His two sons who were also on board watched as their father was taken away. One son got on the radio and falsely told all who were listening that the Marine Patrol Officer had arrested then beat his father while he was handcuffed. The other son went to the stern of the boat and threw the set of shrimp scales Jenkins had brought on board with him into the bay.

The officer on William's boat ordered his sons to pull in the nets and take the shrimp boat back to Apalachicola. Officers Clark and Jenkins followed along behind in their patrol boat with the prisoner.

By the time the boats arrived at the docks, most of the community was there to meet them and everyone was angry from the story they had heard over their radios. When they saw the bloodied and handcuffed Williams they became enraged. He had received a small cut on the bridge of his nose fighting with Officer Jenkins and it had bled onto the front of his t-shirt causing a large red stain. Officer Jenkins and the local Marine Patrol supervisors escorted his prisoner through the crowd into the Sheriff's office while Officer Clark went to a nearby fish camp to take his boat out of the water.

A family member in the crowd claimed that the deaf boat captain had not understood Jenkin's order for him to stop and he was just defending himself from an unknown intruder when he came aboard. The fact that Jenkins was in full uniform evidently did not seem to have registered with the Captain. The townspeople, already angry over the shrimp size regulations were mad as hell at the Florida Marine Patrol and there was no reasoning with them over the incident. A group of fishermen, not knowing where Jenkins, was, decided to seek him out and take their anger out on him.

Officer Clark arrived at the fish camp and was beginning to take his boat out of the water when six vehicles loaded with fishermen pulled up to him looking for Officer Jenkins. When they found he was not there they left and went to the motel where the officers working the detail were staying.

A sleepy officer who had worked the night shift was awakened by a burly fisherman pounding on his door and when he opened it he saw another 30 angry fishermen behind him with guns. They demanded to know where Jenkins was. He told them he did not know what they were talking about and closed the door.

The officer went back into his room and called the office in Carrabelle as the fishermen began breaking out the glass in the motel room's jalousie door. He told the dispatcher of the situation and officers were sent to his assistance. It was decided that all the officers should leave the Apalachicola motels and move to a safer location in Carrabelle. When the officers' vehicles left Apalachicola that day a caravan of trucks with angry fishermen followed them all the way through Eastpoint before turning around.

That night some patrol cars were vandalized and officers were threatened. In response, the Patrol's presence was doubled for the next few weeks while the shrimp were running. Officers found their tires flat when returning to their vehicles at the boat ramp and the locals rode through the ramp area cussing and shouting insults while giving them the finger. Things eventually cooled down when the size of the shrimp rose to a sufficient enough size to open the bay and the officers who had been called in from other areas returned to their homes.

That afternoon, Martin A. Williams was out the front door of the jail before the officers even finished their paperwork. When the case went to the local court for trial a few months later he was acquitted by a jury of his peers.

Williams later sued the agency claiming he was injured during the arrest and could never work again. An investigator was assigned to his case and he soon was able to take video of Mr. Williams climbing all over the rigging of his shrimp boat, verifying he had no such debilitating injuries as he had claimed and the lawsuit was dismissed. Williams tried to bring a federal civil suit against the officers but that, too, was dismissed and the cat and mouse game continued.

It was not until the late 1990s when I was Commander of the Marine Patrol District which handled enforcement in the area that the issue was resolved. Working with shrimpers and the Marine Fisheries Commission, we mapped out a compromise to permanently open or close certain areas in the Bay to shrimping.

St. Vincent Island

St. Vincent Island was named in 1633 by Franciscan Friars after a Spanish martyr of the 4th century.[102] The barrier island is triangular shaped containing 12,300 acres of wetlands, dunes and pines. It is four miles wide on the east end and nine miles long. West Pass separates it from Little St. George on the east and the west end opens to Indian Pass. Prior to discovery by the Spanish, Indians had lived there since 240 A.D.

Many individuals have owned the island. One of the most famous was Ray Pierce, who bought the island in 1908 from former confederate general Edward P. Alexander. Mr. Pierce was in the drug manufacturing business and also manufactured the Pierce Arrow automobile in the early 1900's. He built huts on the island and cut roads across it, then stocked the island with exotic game and used it as a private fishing and hunting preserve.

The Loomis Brothers bought the island in 1948. They also stocked many exotic animals such as the Sambar deer that are still there today. Bought by the Nature Conservancy in 1968, it was later sold to the U.S. Fish and Wildlife Service that made it a National Wildlife Refuge.

The island can be accessed by a boat ferry at the Indian Pass boat ramp. Guided tours are provided on a swamp buggy ride through the refuge.

---

[102] Allen Morris, *Florida Place Names*, 215

CHAPTER SIX- GULF COUNTY TO PANAMA CITY

Gulf County

Gulf County, named after fact that it borders the Gulf of Mexico, is unique in many ways.[103] Besides being a fisherman and hunter's paradise with beautiful beaches and thick woodlands, it is the only county in Florida that operates on two time zones, Eastern and Central. The dividing line in the county is the Intracoastal Waterway, where north of the waterway is Central time, and south is Eastern.

The locals know the times by fast (Eastern) and slow (Central). One could leave Port St. Joe at 7:00 on fast time and arrive in Wewahitchka an hour later where it was still 7:00 on slow time. Needless to say many visitors get confused, arriving at meetings an hour early or an hour late, depending on which way they traveled. Locals take the time zone controversy in stride and especially look forward to New Years Eve when they can celebrate the event twice.

When the area was a major railroad and shipping port it was thought best to operate on Eastern Time as most of Florida is in that time zone. One individual who wanted it to stay that way was local benefactor, Edward Ball, who managed the St. Joe Paper Mill, the county's largest employer.[104] Because of his power and local influence he always got his way in the county. Though the mill closed in 1997, a recent attempt to unify the time zones was not successful.

---

[103] Allen Morris, *Florida Place Names*, (Sarasota: Pineapple Press, 1995), 108

[104] Edward Ball was the trustee of the Alfred du Pont estate and a forceful figure in North Florida business and politics.

Gulf County is also unique in that it is one of the few remaining areas in North Florida where one can actually drive a vehicle on the beach. A permit is required from the county but once procured it opens the door to a whole new beach experience. As a warning, don't try it without a permit as the fines are steep.

Indian Pass

On the eastern end of the county, located across from St. Vincent Island is Indian Pass. The area is famous for its great raw oysters. The McNeils, a pioneer Gulf county family, has run a popular raw oyster bar located on highway C-30 for the past thirty years. The building housing the raw bar is an old turpentine commissary-company store built in 1903. A weathered painting of an Indian chief looks out from atop the store, popular today to bikers and yuppies alike.

It was at Indian Pass where I saw my first blue crab jubilee, a rare occurrence. I had heard of lobster jubilees when I worked in South Florida but had never witnessed one. A jubilee occurs when there are low levels of dissolved oxygen in the water. Hundreds of crabs literally crawl on top of one another to get out of the water onto land. They can be seen in piles in the shallow water along the beach. Seeing all the crabs in the water, I got a dip net and a cooler and walked an area of about 50 yards up and down the beach catching crabs. The cooler was filled in ten minutes with large bluish crabs. I took them home and invited my neighbors over to enjoy a hearty meal of fried crab claws, boiled crabs, hushpuppies, slaw and cheese grits. You can't beat fresh Florida seafood for dinner.

At the Indian Pass boat ramp, a ferry will take tourists across the waterway to St. Vincent Island. Tourists go to the island to take the swamp buggy tour in hopes of spotting exotic animals located there. My wife and daughter took the tour once and had a great time. When they returned home they were so dusty and dirty from the ride that the only clean place on them was the outline of the goggles they had worn to protect their eyes as they rode atop the buggy.

Cape San Blas Eagle, photo by Winston Melvin

Cape San Blas

Cape San Blas was named after a Kemetian Bishop who was deported by Constantius, Emperor of Rome (293-306 A.D.) for fighting for and preaching the Nicene Creed. The area was originally called Cape San Plaise.[105]

---

[105] Allen Morris, *Florida Place Names*, 43

Cape San Blas today is made up of two parts. If you were to think of the area as your left arm, the Cape runs from the shoulder at Indian Pass to the elbow (Stump Hole), then the forearm is the St. Joe Peninsula which runs to the mouth of the bay.

Four lighthouses have been built on the Cape. The first was built in 1849 but was destroyed by a hurricane in 1851. Another lighthouse was erected in 1857 but suffered damages from Union troops in the Civil War. To protect the lens and tools they were removed and hidden in Apalachicola; the lighthouse was returned to service in 1865. Erosion soon threatened so it was decided in 1890 to erect a 98 foot tower 1500 feet further inland. Once again erosion threatened the new tower, so it was moved a quarter mile inland in 1918.

The lighthouse was deactivated from service as a navigational aid in 1996. Erosion once again threatened the lighthouse so it was decided in July of 2014 to move it to George Core Park in Port St. Joe. Today the lighthouse and restored keepers cottages serve as a tourist spot where tourists can go once a month, on a full moon, to climb the tower and view the gulf and St. Joe Bay.

I bought a beach house on Cape San Blas in 1994 and lived and worked in the area for eight years, commuting each day to the Florida Marine Patrol headquarters office in Panama City. My district covered the area from Pensacola to the Suwannee River so it was good to have a place to live in the middle of the area. Now it is used as a retirement home where my wife and I can enjoy the white sandy beaches that were voted the best in the world. One can relax and watch beautiful sunsets, horseback riders on the beach, and hawks and eagles soaring in the sky while stingrays and dolphins feed in the surf.

Catfish Pearls

If visiting Gulf County one happens to be walking on the beach at Cape San Blas and sees a woman wearing a floppy hat carrying a hatchet, don't be afraid — she's just my wife. She is continuing a family tradition passed on from her grandmother. No-- it was not axe-murderess. As a child she taught her how to find catfish pearls. The hatchet is used to extract them. "O.K.," you might be thinking, "I'll bite, what the hell are you talking about?"

A catfish pearl is really an otolith or ear stone, part of the inner ear of the catfish. It is a white oval shaped calcium deposit with its overall size dependent on the size of the catfish. When my wife visited her Grandmom Hitchens in Ft. Myers, they would go to the beach in search of dead topsail catfish left by fishermen. Finding one, they'd split the head open and dig around on each side to get the white pearls inside. Many people have probably seen what is known as a "crucifix bone"lying on the beach. It really is a topsail catfish skull that's been naturally preserved. When you pick it up and shake it, it rattles. What you're hearing are the catfish pearls inside.

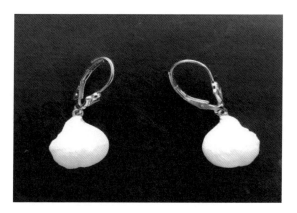

My wife brings the pearls home, puts them in alcohol to clean them and then they're used to make earrings, cards and decorations. Fresh catfish are preferred as the longer they stay in a decomposing skull, they take on a yellowish tint around the edges. It's a pleasure to give one to someone who has grown up around the coast yet has never known about them.

St. Joseph Bay

There are many jewels on the forgotten coast but St. Joseph's Bay is the crown jewel. The clear pristine waters, not influenced by any freshwater inflow, teem with schools of mullet, redfish, flounder and trout. Sea turtles glide through the water as ancient horseshoe crabs bury themselves on the sandy shores and scallops hide in the sea grasses. Fishermen come year-round to fish these waters. During the July-September scallop season, boaters launch their vessels at Presnell's in Simmons Bayou and the city boat ramp near Maddox Park.

Commercial fishermen guide recreational fishermen in the off-season, then during the mullet and pompano runs in the fall, they turn their attention to the more serious business of making a living. Eco-tours have become popular, with Dan and Debbie Van Vleet, who guide tourists from their Happy Ours Kayak and Canoe rental business on the Cape. One can rent a kayak or canoe and spend the day on the bay paddling out to Blacks Island to see the rusty cannons or along the shore to take pictures of baby eaglets in their nests. The bay, most of which has become an aquatic preserve, supports them all.

Another resident in the bay and surrounding waters is the shark. I had a friend in Port St. Joe who used to kid about water skiers in the bay saying, "If people knew how many big sharks are out there they wouldn't ski, all they're doing is being trolled as bait for the sharks!"

Fishermen catch big sharks off the lighthouse point at Cape San Blas and a little further north in East Pass off

Panama City. Flying over the area in a helicopter once, I saw sharks 12 feet and larger in the shallow waters. But other than the mighty Port St. Joe Sharks football team beating opponents, there have been few reported shark attacks in the area. Sharks, like fish, are just part of the ecosystem.

Fort Crevecoeur

Though the Spanish ruled Florida, it was the French who built and occupied a fort on the banks of St. Joseph's Bay in May of 1718.

Coming into St. Joseph's Bay, they constructed a stockade on the main land across from St. Joseph's Point. The fort was called Fort Crevecoeur which is French for broken heart.[106] I can imagine that was how the soldiers stationed there felt so far away from home.

Soon the Spanish governor of Pensacola protested their intrusion. He sent a ship to take the fort and run the French out of Florida. The French Colonial Council decided the fort was not worth fighting over and abandoned it, after burning it to the ground. The Spanish sailed into the bay On August 20, 1718 and rebuilt the fort, but it too was later abandoned. This ended the brief occupation of St. Joseph Bay by the French. A marker signifying the location of the fort can be found at St. Joe Beach on U.S. 98 at Columbus Street.

---

[106] Michael Wisenbaker, " Florida's Other Cape," *Florida Living*, January 1992

St. Joseph / Port St Joe

The town of St. Joseph took its name from the bordering bay, named as early as 1562 by Spanish explorers after Joseph, husband of the Virgin Mary, mother of Jesus.[107]

The original town was founded in 1829 as a result of people moving away from Apalachicola. There had been a dispute over who held title to the lands where they had built their homes. One side argued they had title from the Forbes Land Company before Florida became a state, while the successors, The Apalachicola Land Company, argued the sales were illegal. The issue went to the U.S. Supreme Court who ruled in favor of the land company. The ruling caused Florida's first land boom in the area. Rather than pay exorbitant prices to the Apalachicola Land Company many residents decided to build another port city outside the disputed area.

The settlers (called Saints) established St. Joseph to rival the shipping industry of Apalachicola. Blessed with the deepest port between Pensacola and Key West, the area soon thrived, growing to a population of 4,000. The first constitutional convention held to draft a document for Florida to become a state was held here in 1838.

St. Joseph came to be known as Florida's first resort town as cruise ships brought tourists from southern cities such as Charleston and New Orleans. Prominent Florida citizens and politicians also came to enjoy the grand hotels, beaches, gambling, horse racing, and houses of prostitution. Because of its reputation as a place of where people went indulge their vices, St. Joseph was soon labeled the wickedest city in the southeast.

A yellow fever epidemic, brought by a crewmember aboard a merchant ship in 1841 soon killed 75% of the town's residents and visitors. People dismantled their

---

[107] Allen Morris, *Florida Place Names*, 213

houses and moved away in droves in fear of the plague, many returning to Apalachicola. Fire and a destructive hurricane the following year, effectively ended the town's boom.

In 1844 another hurricane wiped out what was left of St Joseph. It was not until 1909 that the town of Port St. Joseph was established. By an act of the legislature the town's name was changed to Port St. Joe on March 10, 1910.

"The Joe"

Locals in Port St. Joe refer to their town at "The Joe," such as "how long have you lived in the Joe," or "I think I'll go shopping in the Joe." Conversely if they were going to go out to the beach it was referred to as going to the "Cape" or if traveling up to Wewahitchka they say "Wewa." This economy of language saves having to waste time and words. Stores are referred to as "the Pig" for the Piggly Wiggly or "Igga" for the IGA.

People in Apalachicola are the same, referring to the town as "Apalach" and their grocery as "the Rabbit" for the Red Rabbit store there.

I was in the Rabbit one evening buying groceries and a man was standing behind me, he had no grocery cart or items in his hands so the cashier asked him what he was in line for saying "Do you want to buy cigarettes?"
"Oh no," replied the man "I've got gas."
Everyone just stood there kind of awkwardly until the cashier, realizing he meant he had *bought* gas from the pump outside and just wanted to pay for it, referred him to the counter at the other end of the store. Either way, I was glad when he left, whether he was buying or passing gas.

Judgment Day

The hot July day in 1987 had started normally enough; Judge W. Lamar Bailey and his wife had left their home in Blountstown and had driven to Port St. Joe in time for him to drop her off at the St. Joe Country Club Golf Course while he went to the courthouse to preside over an alimony hearing.

The judge met with the two lawyers, Tom Ingles, representing Inez Huckeba, and Robert Moore, who represented her husband, Clyde Melvin.[108] Ms. Huckeba's sister, Peggy Paulk, accompanied her as a witness. At 9:00 a.m. all of them gathered in the judge's conference room with a court reporter dutifully taking notes of the proceedings.

The hearing had come about because Ms. Huckeba claimed she had not been receiving her $350 a month alimony payments from Melvin. They had been divorced in November of 1986 and she was trying to move on with her life. He was currently employed as a security guard at the St. Joe Paper Mill and had at one time been a Franklin County Commissioner. Attorney Ingles filed a motion with the judge to hold Mr. Melvin in contempt for failure to make the court ordered payments to his ex-wife. The lawyers made their arguments to the Judge, with both sides accusing the other of issues that really did not have anything to do with whether the payments had been made or not.

Around 10 o'clock the Judge had ruled the matter finished and was preparing to leave the room when suddenly Clyde Melvin pulled out a 357 caliber pistol from his boot and shot at his wife, missing her.[109] Tom Ingles, a

---

[108] "3 Killed, 2 Wounded in Tragedy," *The Star* (Port St. Joe, FL), July 30, 1987.
[109] Ibid.,

twice wounded Vietnam veteran, tried to disarm Melvin and he was shot; as he lay dying from his wounds, everyone else in the room tried to get away from the madman with a gun.

The judge ran to his office and attempted to hide in the bathroom but Melvin went after him. Finding the stall door locked, he fired one shot through it, hitting and killing Judge Bailey.[110] In the next stall his lawyer, Robert Moore, sat crouched and hiding but Melvin was not interested in hurting him.

He went after his wife and her sister and found Peggy Paulk on the stairway leading up to the roof. He shot and killed her there on the stairs.[111] He grabbed his wife and drug her up the stairs to a catwalk that separated the courthouse and the Sheriff's office. By this time lawyer Robert Moore had run over to Sheriff Al Harrison's office shouting that Clyde had pulled out a gun and was shooting people in the courthouse.

Sheriff Harrison went out to his car and retrieved his handgun from the trunk.[112] He and his deputies saw Melvin with his wife in tow on the roof. A small three foot wall surrounded the roof and every now and then they would see his head pop up. Melvin shouted to the Sheriff that he would never get him. Then he pulled his wife up into view, put a 22 derringer pistol to her head and shot her, wounding her in the neck. Following this shooting, he turned the gun towards the Sheriff and his deputies.

Sheriff Harrison took careful aim with his 38 caliber revolver and fired at Melvin, hitting him with his third shot in the left side of his neck.[113] Melvin fell bleeding to the roof bed near his wife. Law enforcement officers

---

[110] Ibid.,
[111] Ibid.,
[112] Ibid.,
[113] Ibid.,

rushed to the rooftop and found the two of them there bleeding and arguing with each other. "I showed you for running around on me," said Clyde. "I never ran around on you" said Inez.[114]

Both were rushed to the Gulf Pines Hospital where Clyde was treated and released the next day to custody of the sheriff and a jail cell. Inez Huckeba survived but three people lay dead in the courthouse, Judge Bailey, Tom Ingles and Peggy Paulk, making July 28, 1987 one of the bloodiest days in the history of Gulf County.

Clyde Melvin stood trial for his murders in September of 1988. The trial had to be moved from Gulf County to Pensacola because so many people knew the victims that an impartial jury could not be found locally.[115] The jury deliberated for six and a half hours before finding him guilty of first degree murder in the shooting death of Judge Bailey and guilty of two counts of second degree murder in the deaths of Ingles and Paulk. He was also found guilty of attempted first degree murder of his ex-wife. The Judge sentenced him to serve four life terms.[116] Clyde Melvin died in prison after serving 19 years of his sentence.

Sheriff Harrison hailed as a hero for his actions that day later had his own troubles. In 1994 he was accused of sexual impropriety with female employees and jail inmates. He was convicted in March 1995 for violating the civil rights of female inmates.[117] Governor Lawton Chiles

---

[114] Ibid.,

[115] Associated Press, " Courthouse Gunman's Trial Moved," Miami *Herald* (Miami, FL) May 19, 1988

[116] United Press International, "Ex- Guard Gets Life For Courthouse Slayings," Miami *Herald* (Miami, FL) October 20, 1988

[117] "Federal Trial Says Harrison Guilty Friday," *The Star* (Port St. Joe, FL), Feb 2, 1995

removed him from office and he was sentenced to a four year, three month prison term.

Clyde Melvin's attorney, Robert Moore, went on to become a Gulf County Judge. I came to know Judge Moore during the years we tried net ban cases in his court. He was a fair man whom I grew to like and respect. He died tragically in 2000 while still serving on the bench, the victim of a one car automobile accident.

Mill Town

From 1938 until its closing in 1998, Port St. Joe was identified by the St. Joe Paper Company mill. Located on the bay just after one crosses over into North Port St. Joe, it was the major employer in Gulf County. The first thing one noted as they came close to the mill was the distinct smell. No matter how they tried to mask the smell, it was distinct, and it was not pleasant. The smell of the mill coupled with chemical odors from the Arizona Chemical plant located just across the street would literally take your breath away if the wind was blowing in your direction.

Most of the town's people were employed by the mill and the jobs paid well. A generation of families had worked at the mill and their children looked forward to careers there as well. I moved to Port St. Joe in 1995, just a few years before the mill shut down. Most of the local businesses needed the mill to balance their cost sheets. From the Flour Mill Bakery located in Jones Homestead to the pulpwood truck drivers, to the multiple banks located on the main road coming into town, all relied on their steady business.

The town moved to the rhythm of the mill's steam whistle which signaled shift changes. Workers clocked in or out to shifts that rotated every 30 days. If one liked to hunt or fish, there was always time after working a shift to roam the woods or bay.

The mills demise started innocently enough, in 1996 there was a shut down that many thought would only last a week or so, but then the days stretched out until an announcement was made that the mill had been sold to another paper company, Florida Coast Paper.

Florida Coast Paper operated the mill until the decline of the container board market made it unprofitable to continue. The mill was shut for good on August 16, 1998. By 2003 the mill had been dismantled and a piece of forgotten coast history passed away into memories.

The Beauty Pageant

(While Womanless Beauty Pageant's are a reality in Gulf County, the events and characters in this story are fictional, made up from composites of the many individuals I have known on the forgotten coast)

In a small town such as Port St. Joe, everyone comes together to support local charities and have a good time. Each October the Port St. Joe Lions Club sponsors a beauty pageant to raise money to help buy glasses for those unable to afford them. The Constitution Hall is used for the affair while local businesses and civic groups chip in to provide advertising and refreshments. The one twist to the pageant is that it was a *womanless* beauty pageant. Local men were cajoled or volunteered by their spouses or bosses to participate. One pageant still stands out in my memory.

The night had started with a fish fry on the grounds, and after dinner everyone hurried into the Constitution Hall to get a seat close to the stage. Sheriff Stanton, Judge Bixby, Shirley Bevin's the head of the local Woman's Club, and Trixie Eller, church secretary at the First Methodist Church, were the judges. Danny Davis, a local radio station disk jockey, served as the master of ceremonies.

Danny warmed the crowd up by doing his impressions. He reeled off ten different personalities but it soon became evident he had only mastered three: John Wayne, James Cagney and Ed Sullivan. Unfortunately all the others sounded like the first three. People cocked their heads when he tried to imitate Marilyn Monroe singing "Happy Birthday" to President Kennedy and it came out sounding like a frog trying to seduce a mob boss. Finally Danny stopped and the high school pep band played the Sharks fight song which everyone sang with gusto. Then it was time for the pageant to begin.

Joe Dodd led off and everyone had to admit that he was one of the prettiest contestants that ever dressed up like a woman, but he was also one of the roughest commercial fishermen in town. He wore a long yellow dress and a small white bonnet. His ample bosom overflowed beneath his tight sweater set off by a string of white pearls. He wore shiny silver stockings and red pumps. Sashaying across the stage, he gave his hips a little wiggle that drew catcalls from the boisterous audience. His makeup was perfect, and bright red lipstick adorned a pouty mouth. Long locks of a blonde wig with ringlets flowed over his shoulders as he stood at the edge of the stage in front of the judges in all his glory, the look in his eyes seemed to say he was available.

Sheriff Elmer Stanton rubbed his eyes and looked again. He could hardly believe that Joe had ever agreed to be in the local womanless beauty pageant, much less appear looking as he did now. Two weeks ago he had arrested Joe for Driving Under the Influence (DUI) when he had passed out at the drive-up window of the local pizza joint. He had to wake him to tell him he was going to jail, and when he did, it took four deputies to wrestle him out of the car, handcuff him and put him in the patrol car. When they got to the jail he wanted to fight again and three more deputies were required to bring him into the "attitude" cell.

It was called the *attitude cell* because it was used to adjust bad attitudes. The prisoner would be stripped to his underwear and placed in a solitary cell that was empty save for a metal chair bolted to the floor. The prisoner was then seated and shackled to a 1 foot chain that was also attached to the floor. Because of the length of the chain the hapless individual would have to sit bending down in the chair. He would be left in that position in total darkness until his attitude got better.

Joe Dodd had been a tough one and it took him all night and part of the next day to adjust his attitude. But when he did, he was crying like a baby and begging the deputies to "please, please let him loose." After the change of attitude was reported, and when the Sheriff felt so inclined, the prisoner was ordered to be hosed off and given a pair of black and white striped prison overalls to wear and then escorted to a cell with the general population. Many a bad character had been in the attitude cell but all came out meek as mice after spending time there.

Joe's snaggle-toothed wife, Dora, was in the audience and she was hollering "Take it off baby, take it off!" but everyone hoped he would not. She had a lazy eye that made me always wonder if she was looking at me or the wall. She had been born second in a set of triplets and likened herself to an Oreo cookie, as "The cream in the middle." Her mother had been a waitress at the Wonder Bar in St. Joe Beach when she met Dora's dad but she never expected her one night stand to produce three children. Joe always swore he got the prettiest one of the bunch even though they were identical.

After the judges had scored Joe, the next contestant came out on the stage. Billy Sacks was the owner of the local paper, the *Beach Town News*. He had never been to college and had just barely finished high school, thanks to the GED program. His dad had managed to get him in the class after he had been kicked out of regular school for getting drunk and driving his truck into the school gymnasium during cheerleading practice.

After finishing school he stayed home to help his father, Billy Sr., put out the paper. When his dad died, Billy took over the paper. His lack of education showed in the weekly paper with many misspelled words and articles that never got to the point. To make up for his writing skills he ran a lot of pictures. One he had been really proud of was a group of cows that were lying in a field dead, the victims of a lightning strike.

Billy was wearing a tight red dress that showed every bulge of fat around his ample middle. He had put two balloons in his bra to give him a bust but one had deflated, so he looked like a misshapen mermaid. He wore his Nikes under his dress and the tattoo of a dagger on his calf peeked out from under his crew socks. He blew kisses to the crowd as he walked across the stage and the men in the audience just shook their heads.

Next up was Snothead Jones. His given name was Tommy but he got nicknamed Snothead in elementary school for his constantly runny nose and high pitched nasal twang. He was from Wewa. Snothead worked for the city as a dog catcher, except his concept of dog-catching was to shoot any stray animal. While many a tourist wondered where their precious wandering canine had gone, it was an effective means of animal control.

Snothead wore a white blouse and a short green skirt that showed off his hairy arms and legs. Wearing a red wig that looked like it had been part of a clowns outfit; he led his pet ferret across the stage on a pink leash. The crowd shouted at him to "get rid of that disgusting thing" and others could be heard asking, "What in the hell is that?"

Cooter Riggs was the next contestant. He was a deputy Sheriff who had been forced to enter by his fellow deputies. Since he was a rookie the short straw had gone to him. He had joined the force after graduating from high school and then attending Gulf Coast Community College's law enforcement training program.

Cooter had wanted to be a cop since he was a kid when he had his mom make up drivers licenses for the neighborhood kids. He would patrol the block on his bike and check their licenses when they were out riding. If they did not have one he made them go home.

He had met his future wife on Cape San Blas where she was vacationing with her family from New York. Theirs was a summer romance that blossomed into love. She was a high society type and a good looker. Moving to Port St. Joe had been a hard thing for her to do but Cooter made it up to her when he bought a small place on the beach where she could spend her time while he worked. Every so often she would return to her parent's home to visit and shop. When she got back to town she was always wearing the latest fashions.

Cooter was a slightly built man and his wife's new frilly pink dress actually fit him well. She had also let him put on her push-up bra from Saks Fifth Avenue that had little red valentine hearts on it. Looking at him in his high heels and make-up some of the guys in the audience whistled and called out to him saying, "Hey, Cooter, how about a date?" Cooter shot them an angry look and walked stiffly across the stage wishing this whole ordeal would end soon.

Ted Dyals was the next beauty. He wore a two piece bathing suit decorated with tiny butterflies. He held a bouquet of flowers and stopped to throw a few to the crowd that shouted in approval. Ronnie Smith wore his wife's wedding gown which was an embarrassment to her, not because he wore it, but because she herself could not fit in it anymore. Willie Houseman wore a Mumu with a large flower print on it and sandals. The last contestant was David Reed who worked at the U.S. Post office. He was dressed in a princess outfit complete with crown and wand. Some of the guys were heard to whisper "I always knew he was a fairy!" as he walked across the stage.

After the judges had scored the beauty part of the contest it was time for the talent show. Not wanting to embarrass the men by making them perform solo, a group number was planned. The manly women formed a chorus line and sang the Shania Twain song, "Man! I feel like a Woman," while the crowd laughed so hard they cried.

The contestants went backstage to await the judge's decision while a slide program of the men getting dressed in their outfits was shown. The crowd buzzed with people talking and laughing about their favorite beauty while the four judges huddled in the back of the room and compared notes.

Joe Dodd peeked out from behind the curtains when the slide show switched from Snothead's to Cooter's preparations, and when he saw a picture of Cooter putting on the red valentine heart bra his blood began to boil. His Dora had a bra just like that from K Mart! He looked around for Cooter, intent on finding out how he got his wife's bra. His emotions swung between rage at Cooter to sorrow that his beautiful Dora would cheat on him. He spied Cooter and flew after him with his fists raised. "Put'em up you bastard," shouted Joe at Cooter. "I'm agonna whip your ass!"

Ted Dyals jumped between the two men telling Joe to "Calm down man," and asked him, "What's the matter?" Joe struggled to get at Cooter saying that "Cooter had sullied his wife's reputation." Cooter looked at him in amazement. First, that anyone would ever want to fool around with Joe's wall-eyed wife, and secondly when Dora was compared to his wife there was no match. "I ain't ever touched your wife" said Cooter. "What made you think of such a thing?" Joe told him he knew he had because he was wearing her K Mart bra. Cooter pulled down his top to reveal the bra, then showed him the tag that read *Saks Fifth Avenue* proving it was not Dora's K Mart knockoff. "Well," said Joe, "I'm watching you buddy and you had better stay away from my baby." Cooter assured him that he would and they both turned and walked away.

Dan Davis started talking into the microphone saying, "Let's get ready to *Rumble!*" which confused everyone in the crowd because it was not boxing night. Dan looked out at the blank stares and decided to try another approach. "Are you ready to crown a Queen?" he asked "Yeah!" the audience shouted back in approval.

Dan called out each contestant by name then they walked to the center of the stage to the crowd's laughter and applause. Sheriff Stanton, carrying a piece of paper in his hand, then came on stage taking the microphone from Dan Davis. "Ladies and gentlemen," he began, "Before we announce a winner let's take time to thank our sponsors, the Lions Club, for such a good night of fun." Members of the club stood up and took a bow then the crowd settled back down. "And"said the Sheriff, "Let's thank these brave contestants for being willing to let us laugh at them tonight." Once again the crowd clapped and whistled. "I hold in my hand the results of the judge's votes and now I would like to introduce tonight's three top finalists. Would Cooter Riggs, Joe Dodd and Ronnie Smith please step forward?" The crowd clapped and cheered as the three finalists stepped out of the line as the other contestants walked off the stage.

The sheriff began again, "Our second runner-up is" the contestants held their breaths and waited. Then the Sheriff said, "Ronnie Smith." Ronnie walked over to the Sheriff and he was handed a $25.00 gift certificate to the Piggly Wiggly. He held it up over his head while the crowd clapped.

Cooter looked at Joe whose face was still flushed from their encounter. He hoped he would lose to the fisherman because all he could think of was all the ribbing he would get back at the Sheriff's office if he won. "Our first runner up is..." said the Sheriff, "the beautiful she-male in the pink dress, Cooter Riggs!' As Cooter walked over to the Sheriff, Joe's wife, Dora, began to celebrate, "My baby is the prettiest woman in the Joe" she shouted. Sheriff Stanton gave his deputy a gift certificate for $50.00 to the Piggly Wiggly and patted him on the back as the crowd clapped.

Joe Dodd grinned at the Sheriff when he announced his name as the night's winner. The pep band played the theme to Jaws as he was presented with a bouquet of roses and a tiara adorned with fake diamonds was pinned to his wig. He walked the stage from one end to the other shaking his hips and waving his roses at the crowd that rewarded him with applause. The sheriff held his hand up for silence and then he presented Joe with the night's grand prize, a gift certificate to the Piggly Wiggly for $100.00 plus a free haircut at Fran's Beauty Shop.

The Lions made over $1,500 dollars that night and everyone had a great time. Joe was so proud of his win that he wore his wig with the crown out fishing for the next week.

Foghorn Leghorn

One of the best things about living in Gulf County is the ability to hunt or fish year round. Because of the seasons, one or the other is always available. In the fall one can either go fishing for redfish or hunting for deer or turkey.

Tommy Davis was an avid budding outdoorsman. He had just turned thirteen and received a double barreled shotgun as his birthday gift. When hunting season opened in November, he could not wait to get into the woods. One cool Saturday morning he dressed in his camouflage gear and picked up his gun. He was planning on hunting turkeys on old man Souter's place outside of town. His dad dropped him off as he went into Wewa to the barbershop, promising to come back to get him about noon.

Tommy was anxious to kill his first turkey and the Souter farm had plenty of good spots to call one up. He put his turkey call in his mouth and gave a few "*put puts*," then using an old set of army binoculars; he surveyed the field for any sign of turkeys. Seeing none, he tried again. Soon he heard a rustling sound in the woods nearby.

His heart beat fast as he slowly turned in the direction of the sound. The sounds started getting louder and he could hear the brush rattling as something moved through it at a fast pace. "What in the world is making that noise?" thought Tommy, "Could it be a deer or maybe a hog?" It certainly made more noise than a turkey would running through the brush. Just when Tommy turned fully to the area where the noise was coming from, he saw something large coming directly at him. It had to be eight feet tall and it was chirping and fussing as it ran to where he had been sitting. "My God," thought Tommy, "it's a giant turkey!"

The giant feathered creature ran up to Tommy and started kicking him with his huge legs. Tommy valiantly tried to shield himself. Forgetting about his gun, he threw up his hands shouting at the bird. "Get away! Get away!" The bird danced around, stomping on Tommy and trying to peck at his head. As the bird shrieked at him, Tommy rolled over and grabbed his shot gun. He raised the gun to his shoulder firing two shots at the bird in rapid succession, watching as it ran off a few yards before crumpling into a pile of feathers.

Tommy got up and reloaded his shotgun, then slowly walked over to the bird. It was not a turkey but a huge emu. It seems the Souters had been raising emus on the farm and one had gotten out of the pen that morning undetected. The bird happened upon Tommy in the woods and apparently decided to take out his pent-up frustrations on him.

Tommy was bruised and battered from the attack but even more worrisome was he did not know how he was going to explain to old man Souter how he had killed one of his birds. Even more perplexing was how he would ever live down the embarrassment of being the one who was hunted instead of the hunter to his friends.

Jellyfish Salad

It has been said that if one lives long enough they will have just about seen everything. Yet I was not prepared to see a five year old boy standing in line at the Subway restaurant wearing a real silk kimono. His grandfather, Gene Raffield, had bought it for him on one of his trips to Japan.

Raffield's Fisheries was a major employer in Port St. Joe and Gene was a kind benefactor to many in the community. The business was owned by his father and his four sons; it had grown from a small local business to an international one. The Raffield's were always on the cutting edge in the fishing business. When markets were hard to find they developed new ones. In the 1970s Raffield's' was in Asia selling mullet roe that helped the fishing community survive when fish prices dropped in the states. Later it was red fish during the "blackened" redfish craze that swept the country, and finally jelly fish that helped keep them afloat.

The Raffield's found a market for the cannon-ball jellyfish, a creature that for years had been considered a nuisance to the shrimping industry. The jellyfish fouled the shrimper's nets and cost them time and lost money as they had to stop and clear their nets. The Raffield's realized that when jellyfish were dried and packaged the

Japanese would buy them for use on their salads, considering them a delicacy.

One thing that always impressed me about commercial fishermen was that, either individually or as a group, they were never afraid to innovate. They'd try marketing a little known fish such as swordfish, or develop a new net design, or sell jellyfish if there was a way to make a living from it. That kind of spirit is what made this country great and we owe a lot to their creativity.

Nicknames

In small towns, everyone eventually gets a nickname. Age and sex aside, people watching one another long enough will come up with a nickname for them. I was looking through an old journal of a fishing town on the forgotten coast and was struck by the nicknames of the fishermen. They made me stop and think about how they came about; names such as Pooter, Crying Shorty, Sandspur, Possum, Three Fingers, Chattahoochee, Wolfman, Fatty, Catfish, Suckerfish, Hurricane Red, Doodle Bug, and Tick all evoked pictures in my mind.

When I was growing up one of the worst things one could ever call a kid was a "Titty-Baby," because it meant that he was a momma's boy and no one ever wanted to be called that around friends. I used to have a friend that as a kid was a Titty-Baby; he always wanted to go wherever his momma went. People said he "stuck to her like glue" and gave him the nickname of "Stick" that stayed with him all his life.

The thing about nicknames is that you only get them from people who know and care about you. In the coastal towns of the forgotten coast the people who knew everything about you also still cared.

Forgotten Coast Holidays

Small towns are good places to live and raise children. Port St. Joe and Wewahitchka (Wewa) are two good examples. To many, family events from fishing to attending baseball and football games, to going to parades, were opportunities to gather for a fun time. When I lived there I enjoyed attending the seasonal events, each one making a new memory.

The Fourth

The 4th of July in Port St. Joe is a treat. The whole town gathers to watch as the fire department shoots the fireworks from a barge over the bay just off Maddox Park. Town folk turn out early and park along each side of highway 98 from Oak Grove to the park. Kids run along the side of the road with sparklers or illuminated wrist bands and necklaces. People sit in the back of trucks on lawn chairs or place them on the ground facing the bay. Some start their celebration early, shooting off their own firecrackers and bottle rockets or having a cook-out on portable grills. Boats gather in the bay a safe distance away from the barge, loaded with revelers to watch the show. Their white anchor lights sparkle on the water as they bob up and down at anchor.

When it gets dark the fireworks display begins. People "Ooh" and "Awe" at the magnificent fireworks. Shooting stars, loud booms and delicate flower shapes shoot forth in the sky in clusters. Off in the distance can be seen the start of the fireworks show in Mexico Beach. The show lasts for about thirty minutes then ends with a glorious finale, a furious display of multiple fireworks all shot off at the same time. The sky is illuminated with shapes and colors of red, blue, silver, green and gold as low, deep booms shake the landscape.

When the fireworks were over, I used to like to sit and watch the crowd leave. Fathers carry sleepy children back to their cars, while mothers will gather up their broods and hurry them across the street to walk home. Some drivers rush to get out on the highway while others will patiently wait for a kind driver to let them in. Headlights flash in all directions. Out on the bay, the Florida Marine Patrol officers, who have been monitoring the boaters, turn on their flashing blue lights. Boats go in every direction and their red, green, and white lights, mixed with the officers flashing blue ones, reflecting on the water and into the darkness give another light show as fascinating as the one that just concluded in the sky.

Halloween

I remember Halloween as another time when kids would dress up and come to downtown Port St. Joe to trick or treat. Local merchants would open their stores to the trick or treaters and the city would be filled with families. Kids in costumes walked down Reid Avenue stopping at each store to get a treat. After everyone had a chance to get their candy, there were refreshments for all, supplied by the merchants. A costume judging was then held with prizes going to the most original in each age group. Supporting their community was important to the businesses and many a family benefited from their generosity.

Thanksgiving

Thanksgiving in Port St. Joe was preceded by a turkey shoot sponsored by the local Veterans of Foreign Wars (VFW). Participants paid a dollar a chance to shoot at a target. The participants lined up about 25 yards away from their targets and took aim, and then all would fire. The targets were inspected by members of the VFW and the shooter with the most pellets in the bull's eye or nearest to it would win a frozen turkey. It reminds me of a turkey shoot I had participated in that was raising funds for the volunteer fire department at the Lake Talquin Fish Camp on the Ochlocknee River when I was a youngster. The only difference was the turkey I won was alive.

I used my father's twelve gage Browning that was almost as tall as I was at the time. There were four of us that wanted to shoot but the firemen said, "Let's wait a few minutes to see if anyone else comes." So we waited. After about fifteen minutes they decided they might as well go ahead as no one had showed up and we were getting antsy. We lined up on the firing line and fired. The shotgun kicked my shoulder so hard it almost knocked me down, but I held on.

The firemen went down and got the four targets and started checking for the best one. Much to my surprise, it was mine. The fireman running the turkey shoot told me to go over to the pen and pick out my live turkey from a group that was just waiting for the winner.

I was so proud to be the one who would supply the Thanksgiving dinner that year. I knew just which turkey I wanted. I pointed to a white turkey saying, "That one." The fireman grabbed the turkey out of the pen, tied twine around its wings and feet, and then handed me my prize. I put it in the back seat of my father's car beside me and we headed for home.

By the time we reached Tallahassee, I had given my turkey a name, "Whitey." One thing you should never do is give something you plan on eating a name. When you do, it becomes like eating kin. Arriving at the house, it was explained to me by my father that he had no intention of keeping a live turkey around till Thanksgiving. Whitey was going to that big turkey heaven in the sky that very day, then the refrigerator until Thanksgiving two days away.

Our neighbor, Hamp Hutchinson, volunteered to handle the task of killing Whitey. We gathered in his back yard with the bird in tow. Hamp got his hatchet and placed Whitey's head on an old oak tree stump that now became a chopping block. Saying he would not need to be tied since he would soon be dead, we took the string off his wings and feet. Hamp raised the hatchet and with one swift chop, lopped of the turkeys head.

He let it go and to our amazement Whitey started running around the yard, slinging blood everywhere. We chased after the headless bird, trying to keep it in the yard. He would bump into one of us and we'd push him into the center of the yard. After about five minutes Whitey slumped on the ground kicking his feet and thrashing around, still slinging blood on us all. Then he died. The turkey, once white and majestic, lay in a heap, its feathers speckled with blood.

Hamp went over and picked up the bird then took it over to the garbage can and started plucking out the feathers. Soon Whitey was reduced to a naked carcass of a turkey like we were used to seeing at the store. He gutted the bird, saving the gizzard, heart and liver for stuffing and gravy. Then he thoroughly washed the bird. My dad took what had been Whitey and put him in our refrigerator to await Thanksgiving.

I had been proud of winning our Thanksgiving dinner, but never expected to have to watch it being prepared. It was even harder seeing Whitey stuffed and cooked lying on the dining room table. Needless to say I didn't eat much turkey that Thanksgiving. If I had realized his fate, I would never have named that bird.

Christmas

The first Christmas parade I ever attended in Wewahitchka (Wewa) left a lasting impression on me of how a community can pull together. Before the parade began, I saw families going into the local grocery store asking for plastic bags. Each child and sometimes the parents came out holding an empty bag, and then went off to their desired spot along the parade route.

The parade started with all the local and county law enforcement vehicles driving down the road with their blue lights flashing and sirens blaring much to the delight of the younger set. Local elected officials were next, smiling and waving and throwing handfuls of candy to the crowd. Children scampered from the side of the road to collect the treats in their plastic bags. The high school band was next and then floats representing local organizations and schools drove by, each pulled by a four wheel drive pickup truck; they, too, were filled with riders who threw more candy to the crowd lining the streets.

The Sheriffs' Mounted Posse was next riding horses that were outfitted in shiny saddles. Some of the horses had their manes and tails braided. A couple of hapless county jail prisoners followed the horses with a scoop shovel and wagon to clean up as necessary.

The last vehicle in the parade was a bright red fire engine. Sitting on top of the fire engine was Santa Claus, waving and throwing candy canes to the children. The kids waved and shouted to Santa that they loved him and not to forget to come see them. Then the parade ended and parents gathered up their kids, each who now had a bag full of candy and headed for home. To some this was their Christmas, save for a stuffed kitten sewn by the local Woman's League or toys donated by local residents and merchants to help a needy family.

Because it was a small town, the local newspaper, the *St. Joe Star*, would run a special *"Letters to Santa"* section the week before Christmas. Often readers were touched by the children's innocence and/or greed that would make one laugh or cry. Children wrote asking for daddy to get a job or be released from jail or a gift for their mother. In response, local civic groups and citizens would pull together to make the children's Christmas merry. In a small town everybody sticks together in good times or bad. People might know one another's business and even talk about them, but they also had a heart of charity for their own.

Panama City

Panama City is simply Panama (pronounced Pan-E-Ma or Pan-A-Maw) by locals. The city was originally named Park Resort then later Harrison. In 1909 when the city was incorporated, founders decided to rename it Panama City in anticipation of the business its port would receive from the soon to be completed Panama Canal. Located on a straight, 1530 mile line from the canal, the city is situated as the first port that cargo ships coming from there would reach in the state.[118]

The Redneck Riviera

For years Panama City Beach has been called the "Redneck Rivera" in reference to the steady influx of tourists from Georgia and Alabama farming communities. They crowd the beaches, arcades, beer joints, water parks, and tattoo parlors. Wearing air-brushed shirts with their names outlined in bright blue, they gather at the buffets, snake farms, go-kart rides and putt-putt golf links. They

---

[118] Allen Morris, *Florida Place Names*, 190

drive pick-ups with whip antennas and rebel flags. In the back of their trucks are lawn chairs and beer coolers, placed there so they can sit, drink, and cat-call at girls in swimsuits as they cruise the beach.

Old retired military men ride Harley motorcycles, their thin gray ponytails showing beneath red bandanas. You can hear someone say "I'm from L.A." when asked where they are from, not referring to Los Angles but "Lower Alabama" with great pride. The beaches are lined with Mom and Pop no-tell motels where a couple of kids will rent one room then try to sneak in 10 or more friends to party and sleep.

Everyone from North Florida, South Georgia or Lower Alabama, no matter if they were born 8 or 80 years ago probably has a memory and a story about going to Panama City Beach for spring break or weekend trips. More than likely drinking was involved, as well as ogling the opposite sex, riding the rides at the Miracle Strip Amusement Park or Petticoat Junction, playing in the water at Shipwreck Island, cruising along the strip while hanging out car windows, riding the elevator to the Top O' the Strip to view the gulf, climbing on motel balconies to get from room to room, and eating fresh doughnuts while watching the sun rise.[119] But like everything else on the Forgotten Coast, things began to change in the 1990s.

In 1995 Hurricane Opal blew into town damaging most of the 50s era motels on the beaches causing them to either be torn down or refurbished. Many looked upon Opal as a good thing in that it brought urban renewal to the area. Some motels closed their doors forever while others sold the land to developers who put up towering condominiums that blocked the beach from view as you drove down the strip.

---

[119]Petticoat Junction closed in 1984. The Top O' the Strip closed in 1995. Shipwreck Island is still in operation.

In September of 2004 the Miracle Strip Park Amusement Park, a mainstay of the beach attractions, with its wooden Star liner roller coaster, the grinning devil's mouth of Dante's Inferno, and the large Abdominal Snowman, closed their doors forever. All signaled a death blow to tradition, and another sign of the changing times.

Unfortunately, after the area was rebuilt, it lost the uniqueness that was Panama City Beach to those who had grown up going there. It still has beautiful beaches and is a great tourist attraction but the old kitsch that made it different from all the rest is gone, save for the memories. But you can still find the rednecks!

Different Directions

I worked in Panama City as a Marine Patrol District Commander, arriving there a few months before Hurricane Opal came to town. One of the first issues we had to address was the animosity between the American and Vietnamese shrimpers.

The point of contention was how the Vietnamese worked their boats. Most were refugees from South Vietnam, relocated to this country by the U.S. government. They were given shrimp boats by the government that were federally documented, which rubbed some of the Americans the wrong way. Most boats were operated by a large extended family that lived and worked together. They ran their shrimping operations 24 hours a day, only stopping when they came into port to change crews, off-load shrimp, restock and re-fuel then go again. You had to admire their hard working attitudes, but most of their competitors did not.

The biggest problem was the way the Vietnamese boat captains fished their nets. They were accustomed to running up and down the coast of Vietnam trawling north and south. The American vessels all trawled their nets east and west along the coast. Many near collisions of vessels occurred and threats were slung back and forth among the fishermen. After many meetings with the Catholic diocese that supported the refugee's efforts, we were able to convince them to trawl their nets east and west as the Americans did.

Not long after things had cooled down from these confrontations, one of my new officers called in to ask if it was illegal to kill seagulls. He was informed that "yes" it was illegal but was questioned further as to why he wanted to know? It turned out that he had boarded a Vietnamese shrimp boat and was checking their catch when he discovered two crates full of dead birds. The crew had been shooting the gulls as they flocked around the boat seeking the waste fish thrown overboard, not knowing it was illegal, they just wanted something else to eat. We explained the laws to all the fishermen again but I must admit that was a new one on me.

CHAPTER SEVEN- TAYLOR COUNTY

PERRY TO STEINHATCHEE

Perry

The city of Perry is named after Florida's fourth Governor, Madison S. Perry. Originally called Rose Head, the name was changed to Perry in 1875. Perry is located in Taylor County which was created from Madison County in 1856. The county was named after President Zachary Taylor.

"Finest People in the World"

Roy Deals Famous Oyster House in Perry. Photo by author

In the 1970s if one went into Roy Deal's Oyster Bar located on the Coastal Highway just outside Perry, the first thing they'd hear was Roy shouting "The finest people in the world come through that door!" Roy and his wife, Rachel, were fixtures in Taylor County and their oyster bar/restaurant was famous for its good food and fresh oysters. I especially remember the small hand-rolled hush puppies they'd serve hot with guava jelly.

Whenever my wife and I ate there, we always hoped that Roy would convince Rachel to play her "instrument." Rachel had what could be called a one woman band instrument that had a tambourine, cymbal, harmonica, whistle, wood block, horn, and bells attached to a pogo stick contraption that she'd play while dancing about the restaurant to the delight of the diners. I later found out that it was named a "stumpf fiddle" after its inventor.

I lived and worked in the area in the late 1970s and even though the Civil Rights Bill had been signed in 1964, many in Taylor County still believed in segregation. Roy felt he had "the right to refuse service to anyone," so he placed a lock on his restaurant door that would only allow it to be opened if he buzzed someone through. If a questionable person came to his door he simply ignored their knocks until they left.

They're Alive!

There was a crab plant located a few miles down the road from Roy Deal's that was run by a man named Willie Fay. He employed crab pickers to clean and pack crabmeat for shipment to markets throughout the southeast. He'd buy crabs from local crabbers and when their harvest was lacking, he'd have crabs shipped in from Louisiana.

One day I received a call from a disgruntled crabber telling me that the shipments of crabs he was receiving were all dead. Florida law requires that the crab be cooked live to prevent any contamination of the meat caused by bacteria which would certainly be present if the crabs were dead and decomposing.

I went to the crab plant to check and while I was there a truckload of crabs arrived. Upon inspecting the load, I found they all appeared dead. Willie Fay advised that they were not dead but in a state of suspended animation caused by quick freezing. He said if I'd just wait and watch the crabs, they would start reviving. I had never heard of such a thing at the time but decided to wait and see what would happen. In a few minutes after being removed from the truck, the crabs started moving! The majority of them eventually did revive but some did not and I advised Willie Fay that those would have to be destroyed. He did not like it but reluctantly agreed.

I started looking at my law book and found that it is illegal to misbrand a product, which, when he put crabs from Louisiana in a can marked a product of Florida, he was breaking the law. I told him I would have to research the law further but to not receive any more shipments until we could clear it up. Once again he reluctantly agreed.

I contacted my office and advised them of what I had discovered and they said they would get with the legal section and let me know what to do next. Two nights later I received a call from a friend of Willie Fay at the Sheriff's office advising me another shipment of crabs was coming in and that he intended to escort it into the plant, daring the Marine Patrol to check them. I called my office and they said to leave the local politics alone and they would deal with the crab house another way.

That same man later became Sheriff. I'd see him again when issues surrounding the "Net Ban" heated up. He was trying to find out ways to help his constituents get around the law. I confronted him about this, since it was such a blatant violation of his oath as a law enforcement officer and he told me *"he was learning how to be a Sheriff"*.

There would be others that compromised their law enforcement and constitutional duties in Taylor county as well, enticed by the lure of quick money in the smuggling of illegal drugs.

Cool Breezes

When I worked for the Florida Marine Patrol in the late 1970s I made friends with the owners of a fish camp near the mouth of Spring Warrior creek. Spring Warrior is located off the gulf coast of Taylor County. Timucua Indians used to live near there and the area is rich in shell mounds and artifacts from arrow heads to pottery shards.

The fish camp was operated by a married couple named Pete and Jerry. Pete rented boats, guided fishing tours and stone crabbed while Jerry kept the books, ran the bait shop and store and had babies. They must have had seven kids and though they eked out a living, times were hard.

I remember going to visit them and throwing a football with the kids who were happy to see anyone who ventured out their way. After playing with the kids awhile, I would buy a soft drink and sit down on a broken kitchen chair under the big cedar trees in front of their store to talk awhile.

If it was an especially hot summer day, Pete would tell me to wait and he would go turn on the "air conditioner." He would get his water hose and spray down the tops of the cedar trees. The water droplets combined with the sea breezes blowing through the tree-tops would create a cool respite from the day. It was a simple method, but it worked. We'd sit and chat about what was going on in the gulf, if the fishing was good, and how the kids were doing, then I would say my goodbyes until the next time. Every time I see the wind blowing through a cedar tree I remember those days.

Hot Now

If traveling through Perry, plan to make the trip in early morning and stop by Johnson's Bakery for doughnuts. Jerry Johnson and his family have a shop located in downtown Perry that has the best apple fritters, twists and doughnuts you will ever eat. They are always fresh and if one gets there early enough, they are still hot. They only make enough to sell each day, so if you're late you might miss out.

The beach road outside of Perry takes you to Adam's Beach, Keaton Beach, Dekel Beach, and Bird Island and then over to Steinhatchee, pronounced "Steen-hatchee" by the locals. Pronounced any other way, the locals immediately know you aren't from around there.

Who is it?

In the 70s, Taylor County was a hotbed for illegal drug smuggling. Popular drop-off points included the boat ramp at the end of the Dallus Creek landing. I once found a dead man floating in the bay near there; ironically, the bay is called Deadman's Bay. His face was swollen and the crabs had eaten his eyelids, lips and ears. He had no identification on him, but he was wearing a shoulder holster without a weapon. He must have had some argument during an off-loading operation and had obviously lost. We turned his body over to the local authorities but I don't think he was ever identified.

Keaton Beach

Keaton Beach is a popular fishing spot for both Florida and Georgia fishermen that was named after an early Taylor County settler. Because of its close proximity, Georgia fishermen come by the hundreds in the trout and scallop seasons. I have spent many a night searching for fishermen lost, broken down, or trapped by outgoing summer tides off Keaton Beach. It was one of those rare places where a boater could be running his boat a mile off-shore and run aground on a mud flat or get a crab trap tangled in his propeller.

The navigation system used by locals is a series of bird racks or roosts that were constructed years earlier. The roosts consisted of perches for the birds and a platform underneath them. The platform was for the purpose of catching their droppings that were used for fertilizer. I am sure you have heard how powerful bird guano is as a fertilizer. Laid out along the coast line offshore, they made great navigational aids for boaters.

When I worked there, a family named Sherman ran the only boat lift and had a bait shrimp business in Keaton Beach. Mr. Sherman and his son assisted me when looking for overdue boats. The elder Sherman died of cancer, but his son continued to run the business for a few years until he could no longer afford to do so. Later a businessman named Shorty, moved in from Georgia and opened another boat lift and store.

Painful Memories

Every fisherman who went out from Keaton Beach at one time or another probably got stuck in the channel going into the gulf. For years, the locals had tried to convince the Army Corp of Engineers to dredge it out but only got the run around. Finally they got the attention of their congressman and he secured the funding and a channel was dredged. To keep it from filling in, a rock jetty was constructed from the shore at the last bend of the channel where boats entered. The channel was great but the jetty proved to be a hazard. A boater coming in too fast would miss the turn and hit the rocks. Many a boat went air-borne and landed either on the rocks or completely out of the water.

I got called to investigate an accident there that involved a man who had been sitting on the bow of the boat when it failed to make the turn. He was ejected from the boat but not before he lost his "family jewels" on the boat cleat he was straddling. It hurts to this day to think about that one.

Don't Fence Me In

Working in Taylor County 1970s, I soon found out that life in a rural county is much different than the Ft. Lauderdale area where I had worked previously.

People always waved when they passed on the highway. They would wave with the hand they used to steer with that was resting on the top of the steering wheel. While usually the wave was a friendly one, there were times when one had to look close to.see if they were waving with all their fingers, or just one.

Taylor County was one of the last Florida counties to enforce a no-fence law. The state legislature in the 1950's had passed a law mandating all cows be fenced, ending the free range of cattle over private and public properties. In Taylor County, however, the law was never liked and therefore never implemented. Cattle roamed out of the woods onto the highways and many tragic accidents were the result. I used to travel to Steinhatchee by way of the beach road from Keaton Beach and, without fail cows wandered into the road.

I was working with Mike Edwards, a Game and Fish Commission (GFC) officer one night and he decided to run the cows off the road using his blue light and siren. He rounded up the cows and tried to run them off the road, but being stupid animals, they just ran straight down the pavement. It must have looked like an old time cattle drive, except the cowpokes were in a marked GFC truck instead of on horseback. I don't think I ever laughed as hard as when we chased those cows down the highway that night.

Steinhatchee River, photo by Author

Steinhatchee

The name Steinhatchee comes from the Muskogee words "akistihatchee." The "ak" meaning (down), "isti" (man) and "hatchee" (creek) or "dead man's creek".[120]

When I first went to Steinhatchee in the late 1970s I found a small fishing village frequented mainly by recreational fishermen from Georgia and local commercial fishermen. The woods around the area were full of beautiful orange Oleander that you will not find growing anywhere in the state below Steinhatchee.

The old fish camps, Pecks Ideal Fish Camp, O'Steens, Misty Waters, and Westwind rented fishing boats and motel rooms. Fishermen came in the fall when the temperatures started dropping and the speckled trout were moving into the river.

---

[120] Allen Morris, *Florida Place Names*, (Sarasota: Pineapple Press), 227

The week before Thanksgiving every year the river was so crowded one could literally walk across the river on the boats. I remember one year everyone was catching fish and happy. Then the commercial fishermen went out to the mouth of the river and struck their gill nets catching thousands of pounds of trout. Instantly the fishing quit and the recreational fishermen got mad.

One thing the recreational fishermen did not realize was that the commercial men were just trying to make a living and feed their families and therefore they had no concern for the recreational fishermen. One thing the commercial men did not realize was that their attitudes and actions helped turn people against them.

In the 70s the market for mullet bottomed out as it does from time to time. New markets were found in Japan by the wholesalers for the fish roe of the mullet that helped the industry survive. Because no one wanted to pay anything for the fish themselves, many were split open for their roe, then dumped. I was called to many a pile of dead fish abandoned in the woods around Steinhatchee during those years. Unfortunately, it was incidents like these that helped proponents of a net ban to pass their amendment.

To cross the river from Steinhatchee to the Jena side one had to travel on the one lane steel swing bridge. If another car was coming across one would have to wait before they could go to the other side. Today the bridge is gone, replaced by a modern structure that allows big boats enough room to pass under.

Festival

We worked in the Steinhatchee community but also joined in when they gathered together to celebrate holidays. This was the case with most of our officers in the early days who were assigned to live in the coastal counties. They were also members of the community, raising their families like everyone else.

Each fall there was a Halloween festival at the community center. Kids dressed up in their costumes and booths were set up for them to win prizes. From tossing bean bags to going fishing for prizes to cake walks, everyone had a good time.

The cake walk was a popular event because there were many great cooks. Fresh cakes were made and decorated then auctioned off by way of a walk. People paid a dollar apiece for a chance at winning the cake. They walked in a circle stepping on numbered squares while music played. When the music stopped they'd stand on a numbered square while the lucky number was drawn out of a hat then called out. If one happened to be on the corresponding square they won the cake. If not they could always try again for the next cake by paying another dollar. Plates of fried fish piled high with hushpuppies, cheese grits and swamp cabbage were sold to raise money for local causes. Everyone always had a good time.

Swamp cabbage, cut from local cabbage palm, was considered a staple in the fishing communities. One could usually buy a stalk of cabbage cut and trimmed at the fish house when purchasing their mullet. It was something one had to acquire a taste for, either they liked it or not. Many thought it too strong flavored for their liking but when cooked right with a little sugar added it can't be beat. Many locals said it was poison to eat swamp cabbage in the summertime. That was only because they did not want to be bothered with the job of cutting down a palm tree in the summer heat.

Stone Crabs

I worked the Steinhatchee area as a Florida Marine Patrol officer with my friends and fellow officers, Gary Jones, and Sergeant Gordon Malloy. Together we were responsible for the area from Cedar Key to Perry.

We used to check the stone crabbers when they came in during the fishing season. Because you have to cook the crab claw before freezing it, (otherwise the meat sticks to the shell) every night when the boats came in they'd boil crab claws to ship to market in the morning. The Philemon's were a commercial fishing family and we considered them friends. At one time they also operated a restaurant on the river called Taylors.

They would come in with their crabs at night and Sergeant Malloy and I would check their catch and sit and talk while they boiled their crab claws. A huge square metal vat, under which a gas cooking element was placed, was filled with water and stone crab claws then brought to a boil. The claws would be classified as one of two types: "full" meaning the meat fully filled out the claw, or "floaters" those whose meat was immature and left space in the shell causing them to float while the full ones stayed on the bottom of the vat. The floaters would be skimmed from the vat as they could not be sold. Usually the family would keep them for personal use.

Sometimes we would sit around the vat and eat fresh, hot stone crab claws with them. It is only by having such fresh seafood that one can tell the difference from that which has been frozen.

Such times were what bonded the commercial fishermen and our officers. Each of us had a job to do but respected the other for making a livelihood. If they knew we were trying to catch them for doing something wrong but were not detected, or even if they were later caught, it was not personal. We could later laugh about it. That was the main difference in the enforcement techniques between the older officers and the newer ones who thought everyone was an outlaw. This was also another factor in the breakdown of our relationships when the net ban came into effect in the 1990s.

Vacation Time

I had an old fisherman friend who had grown up in Steinhatchee. He lived off the yield from the waters and woods of the area. There were times when he lived "high on the hog" and other times when he had to depend on whatever he could kill or catch to feed his family. I remember one stretch of hard times when he told me he had to eat mullet three times a day. But he took it all in stride with a quiet determination and humor saying in those times he was "eating a little lower on the hog."

One afternoon I stopped by to talk and he was clearly agitated at his wife of many years. He fussed and fumed for a while but then told me he had offered to send his wife on a trip to the Ten Thousand Islands off Florida's west coast. I thought that was pretty nice of him since he was so mad at her until he added that his offer was only good if she agreed to spend a month on each of the islands.

City of the Night

When the shrimp were off the Taylor County coast, shrimp fleets from Texas and Louisiana stopped on their way to the Florida Keys to trawl. We initiated nighttime patrols to monitor their activities. We would depart from Steinhatchee about ten o'clock each night to go to where they were trawling.

The night was dark, but off in a distance one could spot the glow of lights that looked like a busy city. Shrimp boats displayed their white and green trawling lights plus the lights on the stern of the vessel to sort the catch. All together these lights lit up the night. Shrimpers could be heard talking on their radios, laughing or cussing at one another, all on the lookout for the Florida Marine Patrol.

When we boarded the first shrimp boat, the word was relayed to the fleet. Registrations, safety equipment, gear, permits and catch would be inspected and, if necessary, an arrest would be made. It never failed that some fugitive from the law would be found hiding on one of the shrimp boats and have to be transported back to shore to the county jail.

It was always a tricky operation to board a shrimp boat as we never knew what reception to expect. Some shrimpers were aggravated that they had to stop operations for an inspection while others invited us to have a cup of coffee. Officers boarding shrimp vessels in the Keys had once been repelled by a crew brandishing fish clubs. Another time fishermen had jumped the boarding officers and started a fight. It was only stopped when an officer fired a machine gun through the boats rigging that sent everyone on board scurrying for cover.

The seas are rolling and we have to time our jump from one boat to another, a dangerous proposition. At night the waters around a shrimp boat teem with sharks feeding on the by-catch that is shoveled overboard. I have seen sharks hit at rags thrown in the water thinking they were fish.

One night we got a call from a shrimp boat asking us to come get a crewmember to transport to the hospital. When we got to the boat we found the crew members huddled around the bow of the boat while a man lay prostrate on the stern.

We tied off our boat, boarded the shrimper and asked the crew what had happened. One said "I don't know. He just started shaking and foaming at the mouth then his arms and legs locked up and he was stiff as a board." Realizing the man had had a seizure, we went to his side to administer first aid. When I told the crew what it was, one looked at me with relief and said "Boy, I sure am glad to hear that, I thought a haint had got inside him!"

You are <u>Not</u> Welcome

Steinhatchee can be a rough town and even as late as the 1980s blacks were not welcome. During the daytime they would be tolerated as repairmen or truck drivers bringing supplies to the fish camps or even fishing, but come nightfall it was not safe. One evening I heard locals bragging of taking a thirty-thirty rifle and shooting a fishing pole out of a black man's hands, then yelling at him to "Get his black ass out of town".

I think it was more a case of ignorance and fear than bigotry. Most of the residents of Steinhatchee at the time never traveled far away from home, some only venturing as far as Perry or Tallahassee before feeling the need to get back to the safety of their home.

Many small town residents felt the same way, opting for the safety of the known. I know when we hired men from some of the small towns they would put in for a transfer as soon as they could either to get out of the "big city" or to be reunited with their wives who would have no part in moving away

Drugs and Intrigue

The 70s were profitable times for drug smugglers on Florida's west coast. Taylor County with its fifty miles of sparsely inhabited coast was a prime spot to offload shrimp boats laden with marijuana from South America. Coupled with hard economic times, many in the fishing communities were enticed with the lure of easy money. Some were initially afraid to get involved out of fear of not being able to get out when they wanted. They later found they could make a few runs and retire if they just kept their mouths shut.

The going price for an off-loader to use his boat and bring in a load was $10,000; this was hard to turn down when everyone else in town seemed to be involved. It turned out that some local law enforcement officers were also involved, providing information on the movements of our personnel and guarding roads leading to offload sites. County officials were implicated from the highest levels of government and law enforcement.

Things got so bad that Gary Jones and I were approached by some fishermen friends to tell us that even though they liked us, if we were to drive up on one of the drug operations they would "leave us lying," meaning we would be killed. We called our supervisors and informed them of the threats and finally got some attention to the rampant drug smuggling in the area.

We filed detailed reports of the different groups operating in the Dixie and Taylor County area, listing crew members, their boats and identifying their recent purchases ranging from new cars and homes to one fisherman going out fishing wearing his expensive alligator hide boots. All of this information was later used to prosecute them for income tax invasion as well as drug smuggling.

A task force was formed with the Florida Department of Law Enforcement and undercover operatives infiltrated the smuggling operations with the help of a smuggler turned informant. Many loads of marijuana were seized from Crystal River to Spring Warrior and the ring was eventually broken up, sending many locals from Steinhatchee to jail. The locals eventually figured out who the informant was and rumor was that, to protect him, a motorcycle accident was staged in Texas. He was supposedly killed, but in truth was really entered into a witness protection program.

Gordon Malloy, my Sergeant with the Florida Marine Patrol, was an integral part of breaking up the drug smuggling in Steinhatchee. He lived there and knew everyone in town. He was a tenacious person who would never quit on anything. Born on the same day as Elvis, we used to call him "the King." He was born with a bad heart and had to have heart surgery in his mid- forties but he never let it slow him down.

When we were working the drug smugglers around Taylor and Dixie Counties, he somehow contracted brucellosis or swine fever. Later we figured he must have gotten it in the woods from contact with an area where infected hogs had been. The fever caused aching in the joints and feelings of weakness which he battled for a couple of years before it was diagnosed.

In the summer of 1978 he was told that the virus was located on the stainless steel heart valve that had been placed in him years earlier. The only way the doctors felt they could stop the disease was to replace the valve. In July of that year he had heart surgery but unfortunately he did not survive the operation. We buried him in a graveyard outside of Steinhatchee with full honors. Col. Joe Brown came and spoke a eulogy for our fallen friend and a 21 gun salute was given before Gary Jones and I presented the flag from his casket to his wife, Marilyn.

Gordon had married Marilyn when she was still a teenager. She had a son from a previous marriage and together they had a son named after Gordon who was called Billy. Gordon was the one who kept the bills paid and the family on an even keel.

After his death I went with Lt. Col John Walker to present a check to Marilyn to help with funeral expenses. Gordon had been a member of our Propeller Club which looked after members' families after their death. I remember at the time worrying about how Marilyn was going to cope with raising her two sons without their father and her minimal life skills. She did not know how to write a check or balance her checkbook and was quite lost. She soon became despondent and moved the family in with a friend.

In late October she seemed to recover and her mood changed. One day she told her friend she wanted to go get her hair done. Her friend left the house that day not knowing it would be the last time she would see her alive. Marilyn got a pistol from her home and walked into the nearby woods and committed suicide, leaving her personal torment and her two children behind. I remember the day well as my daughter was born that evening, mixing the joy of her entering the world with the sorrow of losing two dear friends in such a short time.

The agency tried to help the family by investigating the cause of Gordon's disease to see if it could be considered a job related injury. A veterinarian from St. Vincent Island flew over to Dixie County to meet with me and test some of the wild hogs in the area for brucellosis. I had contacted a local Dixie County man who trapped hogs in the National forest and we went to his hog pen in Lydia to take some blood samples.

I did not know that I would be actively helping him wrestle the hogs but found out pretty quick it was a two man job. We'd catch the hogs and bend their heads back as far as we could to expose their jugular vein area. The veterinarian then stuck a large gage needle in the vein and drew blood. Once the needle was removed, the thick skin would close off the wound. It was like an old time rodeo as the hogs ran squealing and grunting around the pen as we chased them. The samples were tested but came back negative so we could not prove our claim to help the family.

Their son Billy son grew up and later became a corrections officer in the area.

Bud Lite

The people of Steinhatchee were a close knit group but friendly. The town had a rough side that showed itself at night in two local bars, the Crow's Nest, on the Jena side of the river, and Red's, on the Steinhatchee side.

The Crow's Nest was a one room affair with the windows busted out from the many fights that occurred there nightly. There were shutters over them that could be closed during the daytime, but at night they stood open. If one went in they tried to get a seat in a place that offered a quick escape if possible, or if not, protection for your back if it became necessary.

The son of one of our more seasoned officers named Bud had joined the Patrol in early 1990s. His name was also Bud so we took to calling him Bud Lite. As was the custom, new recruits were told where they would be stationed in the last couple of weeks of the academy. Bud Lite was told he would be going to Taylor County.

One long weekend Bud Lite decided to tour his new area and see if he could find a place to live. He went to Perry then traveled down to Steinhatchee to look around. Little did he know that he had never been in such a place in his young life. People there had a saying that you could find out about things "quicker than a New York minute," meaning you will find something out in a hurry, which he did later that day. As a trusting young recruit looking forward to his graduation, he was proud of himself, but being a stranger in town he made some bad choices.

The first was to go into Red's that evening and have a drink. Sitting there he started up a conversation with a man on the stool beside him and found out he was a local who worked in corrections. Bud Lite told him he was going to be the new law in town and felt like he was talking to a friend in arms. What he did not know was the man had no love for the Marine Patrol or its officers.

When Bud Lite went outside the bar he was jumped by three men and beaten. In an effort to get away from them he ran across the street and jumped into the Steinhatchee River thinking he could swim to the other side — mistake number two. He was able to elude the men chasing him but decided to swim down river a ways then flag down help. He got about a quarter mile away and climbed out of the water.

Going back into the road he hailed a car with three women in it. He told them of his plight and asked if they would give him a ride out of the area. What he did not know was that he had stopped the girlfriends of the men who had beaten him and they were out searching for him — mistake number three.

The women told him they would help him then drove straight back to the bar and delivered him to their boyfriends again. Finally some people at the bar pulled his attackers off and gave him some assistance back to his car so he could leave town. With a black eye and bruised ego he returned to the Academy the next morning. We ended up assigning him to another county as we knew he would never have any credibility working in Taylor or Dixie counties.

CHAPTER EIGHT- DIXIE COUNTY

OLD TOWN TO SUWANNEE

Old Town

Old Town was once called Suwannee Old Town. It had been the location of one of the largest Indian villages in North Florida long before the white man came. When Andrew Jackson invaded Spanish Florida in 1818 he captured the village and a British subject named Robert Armbrister. He accused Armbrister of inciting the Indians against the Americans. He was tried, and then shot.

Jackson's actions set off an international incident between the U.S. and Spain that resulted in the Adams-Onis Treaty with Spain that granted Florida to the U.S.

Checking Oysters

Every fall the oyster industry goes into high gear in Florida. Apalachicola, Cedar Key and Suwannee oyster houses begin transporting their catches to market. Those that can be transported by land within an eight hour radius are shipped by semi-trucks, to reach markets closer to the oyster houses, smaller freezer trucks are used.

To harvest oysters for sale they must meet the legal three inch size limit. Oysters are measured along the length of the shell from hinge to lip. When they are purchased by the wholesaler there is an expected 10% of the total catch that may be undersize but the law says they cannot exceed 20% undersize. To ensure that small oysters stay on the bars, the Florida Marine Patrol measured them when they are being harvested on the water. Because it's impossible to check every boat, inspections are also made at oyster houses and on the highways when they are being transported to market.

Every Thursday and Friday during fall the trucks make their runs to supply their retailers so they'll have fresh oysters for sale on the weekends. Trucks coming north or east out of Suwannee or Apalachicola must go through a Department of Transportation "weigh station" to ensure that the loads they were carrying did not exceed road weight limits. We'd go to the weigh stations to check the oyster trucks coming through, pulling them to the side to inspect their catch after they were weighed.

We'd dump out a bag of oysters on a tarp and measure every single one. The legal ones would be put on one side and the illegal on the other. The total catch was counted then the percentage of undersize in the bag would be determined, if they were over 20% undersize, the bag was put aside. The process was repeated and if the count continued to be small, more bags would be checked. If the count started running higher, then we'd issue a ticket to the driver for the undersize bags, seize them as evidence and send him on his way. A court order would be secured to destroy the oysters or if a whole truckload contained undersized oysters it could be sealed and ordered back to its point of origin so the oysters could be put back on the oyster bar to grow.

It got to be a game with the oyster houses and their truck drivers. They would put the bags with the small oysters in the front of the truck and the large ones near the door so only legal size ones would be checked first. Diligent officers would take their sample bags from random locations to thwart this practice and soon it became just another futile attempt to outsmart the officers.

Needless to say the wholesalers did not like us stopping their trucks or coming into the oyster houses to check the catch. They felt that we should check them only on the water. While we did not disagree that the water was the best place to check the size of the oysters, we also felt the dealers had a responsibility to refuse to buy the small oysters, thereby keeping them out of the marketplace. Some dealers tried to act responsibly and some did not so we continued our stops.

When the Florida Marine Patrol merged into the Florida Fish and Wildlife Conservation Commission, the responsibility to check oysters fell to the Florida Department of Agriculture and Consumer Services (DACS) under the reorganization laws. Our mandate became one of working on the water and in the woods.

The DACS did not have the manpower or equipment to regulate the oyster industry on the water, therefore we drafted an agreement which stated we would enforce the oyster laws on the water and they would handle the houses and the highways. Because of their limited manpower, this effectively ended the checking of trucks on the highways, much to the relief of the wholesalers. That's not to say there are larger oysters being sold, only that they are not being checked as closely as the Florida Marine Patrol had done for so many years.

Suwannee

The town of Suwannee really does not consist of much, just a restaurant, fish houses and marinas. It is known as a vacation spot for beach lovers from Gainesville and other inland cities. The size of the area is defined by the number of canals dredged and homes built.

The town gets its name from a Spanish mission located on the river which was called the *"San Juan de Guacara."* The Indians, unable to pronounce San Juan called it *"Seguana"* and from this pronunciation came the name River Seguana or Suwannee River. Others attribute the name to a Creek Indian village called *Suwani* meaning "echo."[121]

When I worked in the area as a Florida Marine Patrol officer, I could travel all the way from Steinhatchee to Suwannee without traveling on a paved road, instead using logging roads cut through piney woods. Drug smugglers also used this route in the seventies to transport their illegal loads around the state weigh stations to avoid detection.

One of the largest loads of marijuana seized in Florida in the 70s was by Sergeant Gordon Malloy off a barge that had been floated into the shallow waters around Suwannee for offloading.

Seven Sisters

The Suwannee area was famous for its tides that came in very high, then left the land bare when it withdrew. One night Gary Jones and I were called out to search for a fisherman who was overdue. Fortunately he had a citizens band (CB) radio on board so we could talk to him. Coming out of the mouth of the river we called him and asked which way he had gone. The fisherman was so confused and disoriented in the pitch black night that he could not remember. We then asked him "if he could see any land nearby?" I will never forget his response "Brother, there is land all the way around me!"

Knowing the only place where that was possible at low tide, we figured he was at Seven Sisters, a group of oyster bars that rise out of the water during low tides forming a ring of dry land. We knew we would not be able to get to him until the tide came back in, so we radioed him telling

---

[121] Allen Morris, *Florida Place Names*, (Sarasota: Pineapple Press), 231

him to just sit tight (he wasn't going anywhere) and we would come as soon as we could. He was one happy camper when we showed up four hours later to tow him back to the marina.

Monkeys

The Suwannee Restaurant was located at the end of the paved road in the town of Suwannee. It was a popular attraction known for its fried shrimp platters. A large group of magnolia trees provided shade for the restaurant and the parking lot around the building. A troop of wild Rhesus monkeys lived in the trees. I never found out how they got there but they had been an attraction to diners for years as they came and went into the restaurant.

Some patrons decided that the monkeys were so cute they would bring leftover hushpuppies to feed them. Even though they were wild, the monkeys knew a good thing when they saw it and readily came out of the trees for a snack.

People took pictures saying how cute the monkeys were, and just when they let down their guard, the monkey would grab whatever they had and scamper up into the trees. It could be a hat, a pair of expensive eyeglasses or sunglasses or even a camera.

The startled victim would try to cajole the monkey down with offers of more food but the furry animal just laughed at them. Often they would break the glasses or throw the camera 50 feet to the ground below to watch it shatter. Other times they just scampered away out of sight. I saw many a frustrated person standing around wondering how they could get their stuff back, the thought of murder slowly growing in their minds. After trying everything they could, the realization that their items were lost dawned on them and they shook their fists, cursed the monkeys, then left.

The monkeys were later removed in the 1980s by Game and Fish Commission personnel that shot them out of the trees with tranquilizer guns. The monkeys were then relocated to Silver Springs in Ocala that hosted another group of monkeys along the Silver River. Since then much controversy has surrounded all the monkeys at Silver Springs. Some wanted them exterminated; others have sought protection for them. I know a lot of Suwannee diners who would support the former.

Cup Oysters

Some of the best oysters I have ever eaten came from the waters off Suwannee and Cedar Key. Gary Jones and I were planning on working a detail one night to check shrimp boats off the coast of Suwannee. We had been invited by the Sheriff to his hunting camp for dinner and since we were not going out till later that night we accepted.

We bought a bag of oysters as our contribution to the meal and while the food was being prepared we put a couple dozen cup oysters on a grill to cook. The campfire steamed the oysters in their own juices and they popped open when they were done. All we had to do was either eat them right out of the shell or transfer one to a cracker and add hot sauce. The taste and smell of the slightly smoked oysters made for a perfect appetizer. My mouth waters even now thinking of that night around the campfire eating oysters.

FRENCH FRIED SHRIMP

1 ½ pounds raw, peeled, de-veined shrimp, fresh or frozen
2 eggs, beaten
1 teaspoon salt
½ cup all purpose flour
½ cup dry bread crumbs
½ teaspoon paprika
Oil for deep frying
Shrimp Cocktail or Tartar sauce
Makes 6 servings

Thaw shrimp if frozen. Combine eggs and salt. Combine
flour, dry bread crumbs and paprika. Dip each shrimp in
egg and then roll in crumb mixture. Fry in a basket in deep
fat at 350 degrees for 2 to 3 minutes or until golden brown.
Drain on absorbent paper. Serve with Shrimp Cocktail or
Tartar Sauce.

Variation: beat together 1 egg, 2 tablespoons evaporated
milk, and 1 teaspoon salt. Dip shrimp in egg mixture and
roll in 1 cup fine cracker crumbs (cracker meal) or fine corn
flake crumbs. Fry in oil or oven fry.

State Archives, Forrest Granger Collection

BATTER FRIED SHRIMP

1 ½ pounds raw, peeled, de-veined shrimp, fresh or frozen
½ cup cooking oil
1 egg beaten
1 cup all purpose flour
½ cup milk
¼ cup water
¾ teaspoon seasoned salt
¼ teaspoon salt
Oil for deep frying (I recommend peanut oil)
Makes 6 servings

Thaw shrimp if frozen. Combine cooking oil and egg; beat well. Add remaining ingredients and stir until well blended. Dip each shrimp in the batter. Drop shrimp in hot oil at 350 degrees and fry for ½ to 1 minute or until golden brown. Remove with slotted spoon; drain on absorbent paper. Serve immediately.

Running Drugs

A lot of illegal drugs came through Suwannee during the 70s and early 80s. Many in town were involved in smuggling and offloading operations. One night we received a call about an airplane that had crashed in the waters off the coast of Suwannee. We went out to investigate and found the plane half submerged in a shallow tidal flat.

There had been reports that someone was heard screaming in the vicinity. We searched in vain for anyone inside or around the plane. I had a dive mask so I put it on and dove into the water that filled the cockpit. It was murky and a slick of airplane fuel floated on the surface. I did not find any bodies, but I did find cardboard boxes filled with Quaaludes, a powerful tranquilizer used by druggies as a hypnotic.

I told Gary what I had found and he started searching for any signs of drugs being stored anywhere. His efforts were soon rewarded with a pile of boxes and marijuana bales stashed on a nearby island. We loaded the drugs onto our patrol boat and took them back into Suwannee.

By this time our investigator and some FDLE agents had arrived and we turned it over to them. We told the local Sheriff what had happened and also that we suspected the operators of the plane were injured and would try to leave the area. Some local informants had given us a description of a suspect vehicle so it was decided to block off all exit points from Suwannee (there is only one road in and out save for the logging road).

Gary and I got in our patrol truck and headed towards Old Town to secure the far end of the road. The Sheriff said he would seal up the town. It always made me wonder about his motives when a few minutes later, I heard him personally giving out a description of the vehicle we were looking for, all the while knowing that everyone in town monitored the sheriff's department radio channels on their scanners.

When we reached Old Town we pulled to the side of the road to watch for any vehicles. Two hours later we saw a car matching the description of the suspected vehicle coming up the highway from Suwannee. We waited until he passed our location then turned on our blue lights and went after him. Turning on the bright lights we could see two occupants inside. I covered the driver's side with my shotgun while Gary approached the passenger side door. We both were on edge and our breath was coming in short gasps as we walked up to the vehicle. We ordered the driver to put the vehicle in park, turn off the engine, and exit slowly. An old man, his hands shaking as much as ours, slowly did as we ordered. Then the passenger was told to exit and his wife slowly got out of the car with her hands up. It turned out they were not the ones we were looking for that night but I doubt any of us will ever forget it.

The next morning I had to go get a Mullet skiff (called locally a "bird-dog") that we had in Crystal River. We used the boat in undercover operations when working gill netters. Because the boat had a broad net platform on the stern, it was decided to use it to bring the drugs out of Suwannee by way of the river. We would transport them up to Fanning Springs where they could be loaded onto a truck to be transferred for storage. That morning I made my one and only drug run, bringing a load of seized Quaaludes and marijuana up the Suwannee River in broad daylight. The funny thing about it was that no one called in anything about a boat loaded with drugs that day.

Canals

The town of Suwannee was built as a vacation and retirement community mainly for harried workers in Alachua County looking for a respite from the city. Canals were dredged to allow access to the Suwannee River and the Gulf of Mexico. Every weekend, from early spring to summer, marina boat lifts were busy with boaters coming and going. Due to the increased boat traffic, "Idle Speed Zones" were created to minimize wake damage to moored boats and the shoreline. Three incidents that occurred in these canals still stand out in my mind.

Cut of Love

The first incident concerned a seven year old girl who had been water skiing. As she attempted to get back into the boat she had slipped under the boat motor. Her father had quickly turned off the engine so she was not cut by the propeller, but he was not quick enough to keep her long hair from becoming entangled in the propeller. Her hair was wrapped tightly in the propeller up to her scalp and because passing boats were causing a wake, ripples of water flowed over her face, submerging her temporarily. Gary Jones and I were in the immediate vicinity and rushed over at the sounds of the parents frantic cries. Her father was attempting to lift the motor out of the water while her mother tried to hold her face out of the water.

We turned on our blue lights and stopped all boat traffic. Soon a circle of boats formed a protective ring around the girl. We got in the water to try to remove her from the clutches of the propeller. It quickly became obvious that we could not get her hair untangled. Consequently the decision was made to cut her hair out of the propeller's grasp before she drowned.

Having only a pocket knife we asked the parents what they wanted to do and her mother said she would handle it. She lovingly cut her little girls locks, all the time reassuring her that she was going to be ok. It took about half an hour and many tears, but soon shouts of joy were heard from the gathered boaters when her father lifted her out of the water. I don't think I will ever forget the panic and joy we all experienced that day.

Docks

The second incident was when I was almost killed one winter night trying to catch an illegal netter in the canals

As gulf water temperatures drop in the fall, black mullet full of roe come into the rivers to spawn. The canals around Suwannee were a favorite place for netters to try and creep in to catch an easy payday. It was most often a local resident who would row out in his small skiff, set his net, then retrieve it and return home before he was detected. Gary Jones had a family member who lived on one of the canals that had a good view of the major area the netters frequented. We quietly set up surveillance there one night.

Gary got to stay in a warm house while Gordon Malloy and I sat in a patrol boat a few canals away waiting for his summons. It was one of those cold, early winter nights when a dense fog slowly settled over the canals. We bundled up against the cold and waited.

About two o'clock, we got a radio call from Gary telling us a netter had just appeared. He watched until the man had set his net and then told us to come fast. Gordon was operating the boat and I was standing beside him peering into the darkness to help navigate the canals. We rounded a bend and somehow found ourselves sliding too close to the river bank. I looked up and there appeared in the fog ahead of us a large boat dock extending into the river. I

224

shouted at Gordon to turn it hard to the left and he jerked the wheel just in time for us to miss running smack into the dock. We continued at full speed up to the spot where the startled netter was.

It took a few minutes for us to stop shaking at our near miss of the dock and I think both of us wondered if catching an illegal mullet netter was really worth the cost. Such thoughts reappeared in later years about some of the tactics that were used by our agency as well as the commercial fishermen when the Net Ban went into effect.

Spray Down

The third incident I recall involved a battle between an old man and a fisherman. Many people have vacation homes in Suwannee that they either visit on the weekends or stay for an entire season. We'd often get complaints from these "implants" as the locals called them about something going on in town they did not think was right.

One fall we were constantly receiving calls from an older gentleman and his wife about fishermen in front of their house. They were under the impression that since they owned the land, they also owned the water in front of their home and they did not want anyone trespassing on their water. Initially our dispatchers tried to explain to the man that he was mistaken in his interpretation of the law. However all that occurred was that a few minutes later his wife would call in the same complaint.

It got to be a constant thing with the man calling in and one day he finally went too far. A fisherman was drifting down the canal behind his house when the old man began to pelt him with spark plugs. The fisherman did not know what was happening at first but then he realized the spark plugs hitting his boat were coming from shore. The old man was screaming at him to, "Get the hell off of my canal before I go and get my gun." Not wanting to escalate the affair any higher, the fisherman left heading to the nearest marina to call the Florida Marine Patrol. When the call came in and the fisherman stated his complaint, dispatchers already knew where to send the officer to check it out.

Officer Bill Cates was patrolling the Suwannee River that day so he was dispatched to go see the man and calm him down. Officer Cates was a big man standing a little over six foot five and weighing around 250 pounds. Usually just his imposing presence got people's attention. Cates eased his boat up the canal behind the old man's house and as he was getting ready to tie his boat off on the dock, he noticed the man was watering his flowers beside the house. Officer Cates called out to the man and he walked over to see what the officer wanted, still holding the hose.

Cates told him that he did not own the canal and he could not stop people from fishing there. He also told him that if the fisherman wanted to press charges, he was going to be arrested.

Something just snapped with the old man, he raised his hand with the hose in it and began to spray the officer in the face. Cates tried to put his hands up to deflect the spray but he was still getting soaked. He shouted to the old man to stop immediately but the man paid him no mind. Jumping out of his boat, Cates grabbed an end of the hose and bent it so the water would stop. When he did, the man's wife came running out of the house with a fishing pole and started hitting him in the back. When Cates let go of the hose to stop the wife's attack, the man started spraying him again. He yelled to his wife to go get his shotgun and Cates knew that this had to stop now. He grabbed the woman and held her in front of him as he approached the man. He did not care that his spray was now hitting his wife and she was screaming at him to stop just like the officer had done earlier.

Cates finally reached the man and grabbed the hose from him. With the wife in one hand and the old man in the other, he stood there looking like a mother holding two young children dangling by their hands as his boat drifted away down the canal. The dispatcher had begun to worry about Cates so she called the Sheriff's department asking them to send a unit to back him up if needed.

The deputy arrived just after Cates had the two in custody. The old man was handcuffed and placed in the deputy's patrol car while the wife was released after a stern talking to by Cates. He really did not want to have to charge either of them, but the old man had taken things too far. Cates' uniform was soaked and his ego was bruised by having an old man get the drop on him. His boat was still floating down the canal to the river and he knew that when this story got out he was going to be the brunt of a lot of kidding. I told him not to worry, nobody would ever know, but now I guess they do. Sorry Bill.

CHAPTER NINE- LEVY COUNTY

Cedar Key

The town of Cedar Key is located on Way Key, one of a cluster of Islands that make up the Cedar Keys. The area was named after the Eastern Red Cedar found in abundance there years ago.[122] It was once the major port for shipping cedar tree wood for use in making pencils as well as palm trees for use in dock pilings. It was said the palms were resistant to worms that infested the wood used to build docks and lasted much longer.

Throughout the years the Islands had been inhabited by the Seminole Indians and used by the Spanish as a watering stop for their treasure ships loaded with gold from Mexico on their way to Spain. Pirates had used the island as a port to launch attacks against ships traveling off the coast. Today the area is a sleepy fishing village and tourist spot for painters and artists looking to find and capture the forgotten coast's landscapes and people.

Shrimper/Crabber Wars

I first visited Cedar Key in the 1970s as a Florida Marine Patrol officer. I remember going there to work a special detail concerning the shrimpers and crabbers.

The crabbers were upset because when the shrimp were running inshore, shrimpers would pull their nets through the area where they had placed their traps, wiping out all their traps. In retaliation the crabbers would put barbed wire in the water to snag and roll up the shrimp nets. One shrimper who was a victim of such an act, retaliated by tying an old car body frame to a crabber's line. When the

---

[122] Allen Morris, *Florida Place Names*, (Sarasota" Pineapple Press), 46

crabber brought the line in with his winch, the car body almost killed him as it came on deck.

We were called in to calm the situation and enforce a line between where the shrimpers could shrimp and the crabbers could set their traps. Each night we would go out and run the shrimpers out of the protected area or "pumpkin patch" as the crabbers called it.

Cecil and Leo

Cecil and Leo Collins were two cousins who worked for the Florida Marine Patrol in Cedar Key. Leo was a "tell it like it is" type person and he never hesitated to tell my partner Gary Jones, and me how we were just a "bunch of boys." We were twenty-five at the time and thought ourselves men, but looking back now, he was right.

Cecil and Leo had the difficult task of working and enforcing marine resource laws in a city they both grew up in that depended on fishing for a living. They would arrest blatant violators but chose to ignore trivial matters such as boats not being registered or not having life jackets on board.

Gary and I were just the opposite, we would arrest anyone for anything — like Leo said, we were boys, not yet able to discern what was important and what was not. Regardless, we always said that if our Sergeant would just let us go into Cedar Key for a week, we could clean the place up.

Not for sale

Cecil's Sunset, photo by author

One evening before going out to patrol the shrimp/crab line, we went to a local seafood restaurant named Johnson's for dinner. The owner had some of the best smoked mullet dip I had ever tasted. I later found out her secret ingredient was pineapple.

After dinner, we were standing on the dock and Cecil Collins, the local Cedar Key officer, pulled up in his patrol boat. He tied his boat off, then sat down on the engine hatch and watched the sun set over the gulf coast while he lit his pipe. He motioned towards the sky that was filled with hues of burning red, orange, pink and purple saying, "No matter how rich a man is he can't buy that." I often think of his statement as I see the forgotten coast starting to be developed.

Smoked Mullet Spread with Pineapple

1 large smoked mullet
3 heaping tablespoons of the following;
Fresh parsley (chopped)
Cream cheese
Crushed pineapple with juice
1 stalk of finely chopped celery (optional)

Mix the cream cheese, parsley and pineapple together in serving bowl.
Flake the smoked mullet meat from the skin and bones then add it to the mixture. Stir well to blend ingredients. Place in refrigerator for 1 hour to chill. Serve with a hearty cracker such as a Ritz®, whole wheat or other fancy cracker. Makes enough for two, but you will want more!

Bud

Cecil had a couple of kids; the youngest was named after him but was called Bud. When Bud had to start in the first grade, he soon decided it was more fun to stay home than go to school. He'd miss the school bus and hide out during the day, then come home when school was supposed to get out. His ruse lasted a couple of days until his mother saw the school teacher at the grocery store and she asked about his health as she had not seen him in class. Although Bud's health was fine prior to his mother finding out about his skipping school, it suffered greatly when she got home.

Because she worked in Bronson and he stayed around Cedar Key, it was decided that Cecil would take Bud to school and insure that he made it into class.

Cecil had to ride Bud in his patrol car as his wife took the family car into town. Class had already started and the kids were settling into their desks when Cecil pulled into the school yard. Most of the kids went to the windows to see what the police car was doing at their school. Cecil got out and walked around to the passenger side to let Bud out of the car. Bud, still trying to avoid going in the building, had one more trick up his sleeve. He locked the passenger side, front and back door, and smirked at his father. Cecil pulled on the door and told him to "open this door right now!" Bud just sat there looking at him. Then Bud's eyes slowly widened in fear as he realized that the driver's side doors were still unlocked. It must have dawned on both of them at the same time because Cecil let go of the door handle and started running to the other side of the car. Bud quickly slid over the seat to reach the locks. Unfortunately for Cecil, his son pushed down the locks just as he was reaching for the handle. The kids in the school house let out a loud cheer for Bud while Cecil slowly steamed.

He threatened, then begged Bud to open the door. But Bud would have none of it; he just sat there laughing at his dad. Seeing that his threats were not working, Cecil told him he was going to go home and get the spare set of keys unless he opened the door "Right now!" Bud still refused; he was committed to his plan and if he could delay the coming whipping a little longer then all the better.

Cecil went into the school building and got the principal to come and stand by the car while he got a ride home to get his spare keys. When he returned, his patrol car was empty. Bud had decided to get out of the car and accompany his principal into school. Bud, knowing his father's temper, decided discretion was the better part of valor. He quickly realized that he would be safer in his classroom than sitting in his dad's patrol car when he returned. Going home that night was going to be a different matter.

"Mr. Henry"

One time another officer did go to Cedar Key and wrote tickets to a bunch of local people while Cecil and Leo were on vacation. Officer Henry Wilson, or as everyone called him "Mr. Henry," was normally assigned to Williston. He was something of an icon to the local kids as he used to ride a skateboard down the school breezeways when he went there to give boating safety talks. The kids thought it was neat to see a 60 year old man riding a skateboard, but when his superiors found out about it they stopped him from doing it again.

Because he was an older officer, everyone in the town and agency respected him. Whenever he stopped a boater they could count on getting a long winded lecture on boating safety from Mr. Henry. But the people of Cedar Key were not too happy with him giving out a bunch of tickets. When he returned the next day, his name, with a curse word attached, was written in paint on every bridge from Chiefland to Cedar Key.

Frying Fish and Politics

When I worked as a Florida Marine Patrol officer in Taylor County, the area headquarters office was in Crystal River. The Director of our agency, Randolph Hodges, had been a State Senator representing the area and was from Cedar Key. Because of his ties to the area we were often called upon to support many political rally's and campaigns.

Hodges was one of the "Pork-chop Gang" a group of powerful North Florida legislators who ran the state for many years before the 1970s reapportionment. Florida politics of the 50s and 60s was different from today. People wanted to see their candidates and the best way for that to happen was to have a fish fry at the local fairgrounds.

The Board of Conservation and later the Department of Natural Resources worked closely with the fishing industry from inspecting and regulating their catch to helping promote their products. Law enforcement officers from the Crystal River office were regularly called upon by the Director to act as cooks for favored politician's "fish fry". A cook wagon was stored at the office and could be transported and manned on a moment's notice anywhere from Pensacola to Gainesville.

Officers arrived at the site early and began preparations. They would help set up tents, tables, chairs and stages. The fish were usually donated by a local fishing organization as well as the groceries to cook the fish and make the hushpuppies, cheese grits and coleslaw. Officers became specialists at different tasks and went about their assignments dutifully.

Sometimes things went smoothly and sometimes they did not. A new officer was assigned to make the grits one night and we soon learned that he had no idea what he was doing. He had doubled the mixture of water to the grits and ended up with a lumpy mess. The problem was what to do with 20 gallons of watery, lumpy grits.

A baseball field was nearby and it was decided to pour them out on the field. A problem occurred when the grits hit the ground; the water seeped leaving a white film on the field. An enterprising officer solved the problem by using a large dip spoon to dig out a little crater then pour some of the grits in the hole. We must have dug a thousand holes in that field. I always wondered what the team thought about a field that looked like it had been home to a bunch of gophers when they went out to play that next spring.

One of Us

Many years later I attended both Cecil's and Leo's funerals. They were buried in the Cedar Key cemetery on their beloved island. First it was Cecil, then a few years later, Leo. I remember the pastor speaking of Leo at the graveside, "Leo was born here, and he met his wife here, got married and raised his family here. He worked here and he died here; he was one of us." What more could be said of any man's life than to be remembered as a part of his community.

EPILOGUE

Bitter Tears

Fishing families are always the first to be hurt when ill winds blow, be it a hurricane, a net ban, or man-made disaster. In April 2010, on "Earth Day" no less, a British Petroleum (BP) oil rig exploded in the Gulf of Mexico fifty miles off the coast of Louisiana. It resulted in the largest oil spill in American history. The world watched as the gulf coast, my Forgotten Coast included, braced for the worst environmental disaster ever to hit our shores. In early June, black globs of crude oil began appearing on the white sands of Pensacola Beach. Everyone felt it was only a matter of time before more oil began washing up in the Forgotten Coast.

Commercial fishermen, already staggering from the younger generation's flight to more stable jobs, competition from farm raised seafood products, and reduced catches; now watched helplessly as their way of life was threatened. The prime in-shore nursery areas, where the juvenile fish, shrimp, oysters and crabs spawn were in danger of being fouled by oil. Federal fishing zones were closed and bag limits are imposed, all draining the fishermen of their livelihoods.

The tourism industry, another staple of commerce for the forgotten coast, also took a hit in the wallet. As soon as vacationers heard of the oil spill on the gulf coast, they cancelled reservations and made plans to go somewhere else, taking along with them the dollars needed to help the coastal economies. Restaurants, bars, water parks and arcades sat empty all summer.

Our coasts could soon have a new, albeit unseen, resident, one that may be here for years to come — tar balls. Tourists swimming in the waters may have to check the bottoms of their feet for tar residue, seeking a bottle of mineral spirits to help scrub it off before putting their shoes back on.

A commercial fisherman, tears welling in his eyes, told me he had grown up loving the taste of salt water on his face, but nowadays it only comes from bitter tears cried in frustration over the fear of a lost love, the Forgotten Coast. I share his fears as well.

This book is written as my remembrance of the Forgotten Coast. It is an invitation to you to come and see the beauty of a way of life that still exists in the people and places where I have lived and worked. Hopefully it will not become a record of what may never be again. The times of crab jubilees and catfish pearls may pass. But I will always have my memories of the forgotten coast. As Cecil Collins said of that beautiful sunset so long ago, "No matter how rich a man is, he can't buy that."

[Authors Note 6/1/15 -Fortunately the environmental damages to the Forgotten Coast have been avoided so far, though many still suffer from the economic losses.]

BIBLIOGRAPHY

Adams, Arthur G. *The Hudson through the Years*, New York: Fordham University Press, 1996

Cash, W.T. *Florida Becomes a State*, Tallahassee: Florida Centennial Commission, 1945.

Drew, Frank. *Florida Place-Names of Indian Origin*, Florida: Florida Historical Society Quarterly, April 1928.

Federal Writers Project, *A Guide to the Southernmost State: Florida*, New York: Oxford University Press, 1944.

Florida State Hotel Commission. *Florida Empire of the Sun*, Tallahassee, 1930

Galgano, Robert C. *Feast of Souls*, New Mexico: University of New Mexico Press, 1970.

Gore, Robert F. *The Gulf of Mexico*, Sarasota: Pineapple Press, 1992.

Hoffman, Paul E. *Florida's Frontiers*, Indiana: Indiana University Press, 2002.

Hopkins, Randal. *Teresa Was Earliest Vacation Spot For Residents After Civil War*, Tallahassee *Democrat*, June 27, 1965.

Johnson, Malcolm B. *Red, White and Bluebloods in Frontier Florida*, Tallahassee: Rotary Clubs of Tallahassee, 1976.

Knott, James R. *Tales of Tallahassee Twice Told and Untold*, 1995.

239

McCarthy, Kevin M. *Apalachicola Bay*, Sarasota: Pineapple Press, 2004.

McLean, Will. Song: *Tate's Hell, 1972*

Milanich, Jerald T. *Florida's Indians from Ancient Times to the Present*, Florida: University Press, 1981.
Morris, Allen. *Florida Place Names*, Florida: Pineapple Press, 1995.

Must See, Must See Media LLC, Port St Joe, Fl, 2009 Vol 3 #1 Spring 2009 *"Myths and Legends of the Forgotten Coast."*

Owens, Harry P. *Apalachicola: The Beginning*, Florida Historical Quarterly Vol 47, July 68-April 69.

Pringle, Rev Ray, Sr. *State Chaplin's Message*, Florida Fishermen's Federation Newsletter, 1995.

Purdum, Elizabeth D. and Fernald, Edward A. *Water Resources Atlas of Florida*, Tallahassee: Florida State University Institute of Science and Public Affairs, 1998.

Read, William A. *Florida Place Names of Indian Origin and Seminole Personal Names*, Louisiana: Louisiana University Press, 1934.

Rogers, William Warren. *Outposts on the Gulf*, Gainesville: University Presses of Florida, 1986.

Simpson, J. Clarence. *A Provisional Gazetteer of Florida Place-Names of Indian Derivation*, Florida: Florida Geological Survey, Special Publication No. 1, 1956.

Wisenbaker, Michael. *Florida's Other Cape*, Florida: Florida Living, January 1992.

Newspapers:
Daytona Beach Morning Journal, Daytona
Miami Herald, Miami
Tallahassee Democrat, Tallahassee
St. Joe Star, Port St Joe
Wakulla News, Crawfordville

Personal Interviews:
Joseph Wesley "Snooky" Barber. Carrabelle: February
2008.